gage Cornerstones

CANADIAN LANGUAGE ARTS

Anthology 6b

gage EDUCATIONAL PUBLISHING COMPANY
A DIVISION OF CANADA PUBLISHING CORPORATION
Vancouver · Calgary · Toronto · London · Halifax

Researchers: Monika Croydon, Monica Kulling, Todd Mercer

Cover Illustration: José Ortega

Acknowledgments

Every reasonable effort has been made to trace ownership of copyrighted material. Information that would enable the publisher to correct any reference or credit in future editions would be appreciated.

We acknowledge the financial support of the Government of Canada through the Book Publishing Industry Development Program for our publishing activities.

7 "I am the creativity" by Alexis De Veaux. © 1993 by Alexis De Veaux. From *Soul Looks Back in Wonder* by Tom Feelings. Used by permission of Dial Books for Young Readers, a division of Penguin Putnam Inc. / 8-15 "Pavlova's Gift" by Maxine Trottier. Illustrations by Victoria Berdichevsky. © 1996. By permission of Stoddart Publishing. / 20-21 "Self-Portrait," text and illustration by George Littlechild from *Just Like Me* edited by Harriet Rohmer. © 1997. By permission of Children's Book Press. / 24-27 "Emily of New Moon" by Lydia Stone from *Kidsworld Magazine* (Winter 1998). / 30 "The Conductor's Hands" by Alice Schertle from *Call Down the Moon* edited by Myra Cohn Livingston. © 1995. Used by permission of the author. / 30 "Taking Violin at School" by April Halprin Wayland from *Cricket Magazine* (April 1995). © 1995 by April Halprin Wayland. Reprinted with permission. / 31 "Choir Tryouts" from *The Great Frog Race* by Kristine O'Connell George. © 1997 by Kristine O'Connell George. Reprinted by permission of Clarion Books/Houghton Mifflin Co. All rights reserved. / 31 "No Static" by Monica Kulling from *Call Down the Moon* edited by Myra Cohn Livingston. © 1995 by Monica Kulling. All rights reserved. Reprinted with permission of Marian Reiner for the author. / 37 "My Hero, Susan Aglukark" by Shawna Tatty from *Courageous Spirits: Aboriginal Heroes of Our Children.* © 1993. By permission of Mokakit Educational Resource. / 40-47 "The Jade Stone" by Aaron Shepard from *Stories on Stage: Scripts for Reader's Theatre.* Adapted from *The Jade Stone* by Caryn Yacowitz, published by Holiday House. © 1992 by Caryn Yocowitz. Reprinted by permission of Curtis Brown, Ltd. / 50 "Big Words, Strong Words: Martin Luther King, Jr" by Bobbi Katz. © 1998 by Bobbi Katz. By permission of Bobbi Katz. / 53 "Summer Vacation" by Beverley Brenna from *Do Whales Jump at Night?* edited by Florence McNeil. © 1990. Reprinted by permission of the author. / 68-75 "Chris and Sandy" by Monica Hughes. Reprinted by permission of the Pamela Paul Agency Inc. / 78-80 "Robot Critters." Adapted from "Robo Explorers" by Steve Miller and "Robots Inside" by Jim O'Leary from *Odyssey: Adventures in Science* (December 1997). © 1997 by Cobblestone Publishing Company. Reprinted by permission of the publisher. / 84-87 "Spaced-Out Food" adapted from *On the Shuttle: Eight Days in Space* by Barbara Bondar with Dr. Roberta Bondar. © 1993. Reprinted with permission of Owl Magazine. / 90 "Unique" by Adrian Rumble from *Spaceways: An Anthology of Space Poetry* edited by John Foster. / 93 "If You Want to See" from *Reach for the Moon* by Samantha Abeel. By permission of Pfeifer-Hamilton Publishers. / 104-107 Adapted from "The Painted Caves of Altamira" by Joy Hollamby-Lane from the Canadian Children's Annual. / 110 "Fossils" from *Something New Begins: New and Selected Poems* by Lilian Moore. © 1982 by Lilian Moore. Reprinted by permission of Marian Reiner for the author. / 112-115 "Pioneer Geologist" from *Yesterday's Children* by Joyce Barkhouse. Reprinted by permission of Nimbus Publishing. / 118-122 Excerpted from *I am the Mummy Heb-Nefert* by Eve Bunting. Illustrations by David Christiana. Text © 1997 by Eve Bunting. Illustrations © 1997 by David Christiana. By permission of Tundra Books. / 122-123 "How Mummies Were Made." Text and illustrations by Nicholas Reeves. By permission of Scholastic/Madison Press. / 126-131 Excerpts from *Discovering the Iceman* by Shelley Tanaka. By permission of Scholastic/Madison Press. / 140-149 "A Wish Named Arnold" by Charles de Lint from *Spaceships and Spells* edited by Jane Yolen, Martin H. Greenberg, and Charles G. Waugh. © 1987 by Charles de Lint. Reprinted by permission of the author. / 152-157 "Lightning Strikes at the Van Gogh Café" adapted from *The Van Gogh Cafe* by Cynthia Rylant. © 1995 by Cynthia Rylant. Reprinted by permission of Harcourt Brace & Company.

Photo Credits
9 Dave Starrett; 15 Corbis-Bettmann; 17 **Courtesy of the** National Ballet of Canada Archives; 18 Maxine Trottier; 19 Stoddart Kids; 20-21 Children's Book Press; 23 **top** Musee d'Orsay, Paris, France/Eric Lessing/Art Resource, NY (S0010516), **middle** The Artist, Toronto. Courtesy The Isaacs Gallery, **bottom** National Museum of American Art, Washington, D.C. (1967.57.30)/Art Resource, NY (S0044073); 24-25, 26 **top right, 27 bottom** Salter Street Films from the television series "Emily of New Moon," a co-production of Salter Street Films and Cinar Films; 26 **middle left** L.M. Montgomery Collection, Archival and Special Collections, University of Guelph Library; 30 **top right** Andy Sax/Tony Stone Images, **middle left** Mark Tomalty/Masterfile, **bottom right** Clark Weinberg/Image Bank; 31 **top** Richard Price/First Light, **bottom left** Jim Craigmyle/Masterfile; 34 CP Photo, 1996, The Kingston Whig-Standard/Eric Wynne; 36 CP Photo/Dave Buston, 1995; 39 **left, middle, right** Robert Semeniuk/First Light; 50 UPI/Corbis-Bettmann; 78-79 National Geographic/Mark W. Tilden/© 1997 George Steinmetz/213.871.2295; 80 **left** National Geographic/© 1997 George Steinmetz/213.871.2295, **right** Donna Coveney/MIT; 81 **top left, top right, bottom left, bottom right** UPI/Corbis-Bettmann; 82 **left, right, bottom** The Kobal Collection; 88 Mike Agliolo, Science Source/Photo Researchers; 89 **top** Space Frontiers-TCL/Masterfile, **bottom** Agence France Presse/Corbis-Bettmann; 90 F. Zullo, Science Source/Photo Researchers; 92-93 Michael Alberstadt; 98 Mon Tresor/First Light; 99 **top** Paul G. Adam/Publiphoto, **bottom** UPI/Corbis-Bettmann; 100 **top** World Photo/First Light, **bottom** D. Ball/Publiphoto; 101 **top** Ken Straiton/First Light; 103 **top** Y. Derome/ Publiphoto, **middle** Richard Hartimer/First Light, **bottom right** P. Hattenberger/Publiphoto; 108 **top, middle, bottom** The Kobal Collection; 109 A.E. Sirulniko/First Light; 112 John William Dawson, Reproduction of a painting by J.A. Harris. McGill University Archives PR000260; 117 **left, right** O. Louis Mazzatental/National Geographic Society; 125 **left, middle, right** The Granger Collection; 126 Erika and Helmut Simon; 128 **left** Sygma, **top right, bottom right** Rex Features London/Ponopresse Internationale Inc.; 131 Werner Nosko/© SNS Pressebild; 159 **top** © 1996 Universal City Studios, Inc./The Kobal Collection, **middle** The Kobal Collection, **bottom** © 1997 Polygram Films/The Kobal Collection.

Illustrations
7 Michael Herman; 26 **bottom left** The Osborne Collection of Early Children's Books, Toronto Public Library; 27 Dover Publications Inc.; 29, 55, 76-77 Bill Suddick; 33 Steve Attoe; 37 Charles Weiss; 48-49 Harvey Chan; 52-53 Jimminy Roux; 57 **right,** 60 **right,** 61 **top right,** 61 **bottom right** Rose Zgodzinski; 62 Brian Hughes; 63 Steve Attoe; 67, 83, 133 Dayle Dodwell; 111 Royal Tyrrell Museum, Drumheller, Alberta; 112-115 David Bathurst; 126 Laurie McGaw; 129, 130-131 Jack McMaster; 134-135 From *Tuesday* by David Wiesner. © 1991 by David Wiesner. Reprinted by permission of Clarion Books/Houghton Mifflin Company. All rights reserved; 136 **bottom left** First Harcourt Brace Young Classics edition 1998, **middle** W.H. Walker, John Lane, the Bodley Head; 136-137 Kimberly Bulcken Root, Holiday House; 137 **middle** Harcourt Brace & Company, First Magic Carpet Books edition 1996, **bottom left** Annick Press Ltd., **bottom right** Trina Schart Hyman, Hodder and Stoughton, Ltd.; 138 **top left** Scholastic Inc., **right** © 1994 Frances Tyrrell, Scholastic Canada, Ltd. **bottom left** Pauline Baynes, HarperCollins; 139 David Day; 151 Mike Martchenko.

Canadian Cataloguing in Publication Data

Main entry under title:

Gage cornerstones: Canadian language arts. Anthology, 6b

Writing team: Christine McClymont, et al.
ISBN 0-7715-1217-1

1. Readers (Elementary).   I. McClymont, Christine.
II. Title: Cornerstones: Canadian language arts.
III. Title: Anthology, 6b

PE1121.G27 1998   428.6   C98-932139-8

ISBN 0-7715-**1217**-1
2 3 4 5 6 BP 03 02 01 00 99
Printed and bound in Canada.

Cornerstones Development Team

HERE ARE THE PEOPLE WHO WORKED HARD TO MAKE THIS BOOK EXCITING FOR YOU!

WRITING TEAM

Christine McClymont
Patrick Lashmar
Dennis Strauss
Patricia FitzGerald-Chesterman
Cam Colville
Robert Cutting
Stephen Hurley
Luigi Iannacci
Oksana Kuryliw
Caroline Lutyk

GAGE EDITORIAL

Joe Banel
Rivka Cranley
Elizabeth Long
David MacDonald
Evelyn Maksimovich
Diane Robitaille
Darleen Rotozinski
Jennifer Stokes
Carol Waldock

GAGE PRODUCTION

Anna Kress
Bev Crann

DESIGN, ART DIRECTION & ELECTRONIC ASSEMBLY

Pronk&Associates

ADVISORY TEAM

Connie Fehr Burnaby SD, BC
Elizabeth Sparks Delta SD, BC
John Harrison Burnaby SD, BC
Joan Alexander St. Albert PSSD, AB
Carol Germyn Calgary B of E, AB
Cathy Sitko Edmonton Catholic SD, AB
Laura Haight Saskatoon SD, SK
Linda Nosbush Prince Albert SD, SK
Linda Tysowski Saskatoon PSD, SK
Maureen Rodniski Winnipeg SD, MB
Cathy Saytar Dufferin-Peel CDSB, ON
Jan Adams Thames Valley DSB, ON
Linda Ross Thames Valley DSB, ON
John Cassano York Region DSB, ON
Carollynn Desjardins Nippissing-Parry Sound
    CDSB, ON
David Hodgkinson Waterloo Region DSB, ON
Michelle Longlade Halton CDSB, ON
Sharon Morris Toronto CDSB, ON
Heather Sheehan Toronto CDSB, ON
Ruth Scott Brock University, ON
Elizabeth Thorn Nipissing University, ON
Jane Abernethy Chipman & Fredericton SD, NB
Darlene Whitehouse-Sheehan Chipman &
    Fredericton SD, NB
Carol Chandler Halifax Regional SB, NS
Martin MacDonald Strait Regional SB, NS
Ray Doiron University of PEI, PE
Robert Dawe Avalon East SD, NF
Margaret Ryall Avalon East SD, NF

Contents

Into the SPOTLIGHT

I am the creativity

Poem by Alexis De Veaux

I am the dance step
of the paintbrush singing
I am the sculpture
of the song
the flame breath
of words
giving new life to paper
yes, I am the creativity
that never dies
I am the creativity
keeping my people
alive

BEFORE READING

Have you discovered your special talent or gift? What do you do to nurture it? Have you ever had the opportunity of sharing it with others? As you read, think about Pavlova's gift and how she shares it.

Glossary

czar: the title of the former emperors of Russia

Babushka: in Russia, it's a polite form of address when speaking to an elderly woman

balalaika: a Russian musical instrument that looks like a guitar

hemophilia: a medical condition in which a person's blood does not clot normally

Pavlova's Gift

STORY BY
Maxine Trottier

ILLUSTRATIONS BY
Victoria Berdichevsky

Anna Pavlova was once the greatest ballerina in Russia. People had watched her dance on every stage in the country. Now though, she seldom performed in public.

Alone before the mirrors in her ballroom, she would lift her slender arms, rise onto her toes, and with the music, she would begin. Her reflection, a graceful shadow of the young dancer she had once been, would float across the room.

One night, a royal messenger brought a letter to Anna. It said: *Madame Pavlova, I ask that you come to the palace tonight and dance for Prince Alexis. He is gravely ill. It is my hope that the beauty of your dancing will help my son.* The letter was signed by Czar Nicholas, himself.

Not even the greatest ballerina in Russia could ignore such a request.

Thinking only of the ailing young prince, Anna Pavlova put aside her fear of performing. She pulled a hooded cloak over her dress and stepped into the cold.

Her sleigh waited in the street. Near it stood an old gypsy woman. A carved wooden heart hung on a red cord around the gypsy's neck.

"May I tell your future, Madame Pavlova?" asked the old woman.

"No need, Babushka," answered Anna, getting into her sleigh. "My future is behind me."

"Still, I see that you have a kind soul," said the old woman. "Yours is the gift of dance. Look into your own face tonight and choose how to give it." She took the wooden heart from around her neck and pressed it into Anna Pavlova's hand. Without another word, the gypsy drifted away into the snowy night.

With jingling bells, the sleigh began to move. The frozen road rang beneath the horse's hooves as the sleigh glided into the forest. The night rushed past.

Then, with a bump and the squeal of bending metal, the sleigh tilted and stopped.

"It is the runner, Madame," said the driver. "You must step out while I repair it."

Anna climbed down as the snow fell around her. In the stillness, she heard a clear note rise and drift up to the stars. She followed the music deep into the woods until she came to a ring of painted wagons circling a fire.

An old gypsy man played his flute while a young woman danced to the sad, sweet music. Her long hair swung and the gold loops of her earrings sparkled in the firelight.

Anna Pavlova drew close to the young woman. For a moment she thought she was staring into the mirrors of her ballroom. Looking past the gypsy skirt and bright ribbons, she saw herself as she had once been. She remembered dancing the ballet for the first time. Instead of the forest, veiled in snow, Anna could see the endless stage with its heavy, velvet curtains. For a heartbeat, the thunder of applause filled her ears.

"Are you lost, Madame?" the young woman asked, for even she had recognized the greatest ballerina in Russia.

"No," answered Anna Pavlova. "I do not believe I am."

"I will take you back to the road," said the young woman, leading the way.

They stopped just inside the woods.

"How wonderful it must be to dance as you do," said the young woman. "To dance like that, even once, would be glorious."

"Do you wish to?" asked Anna. "I can give you the chance."

"How?" asked the young woman breathlessly.

"Go to the Czar's palace and dance in my place. Dance exactly as you did in the forest. Your youth and spirit will do far more for the little prince than I ever could."

Anna removed her cloak. She swirled it around the young woman, pulling the hood down over her face. Then, without thinking, she took off the wooden heart and placed it around the gypsy's neck.

The sleigh stood ready. The young woman ran to it and when she was inside, it whispered off into the dark.

Anna Pavlova walked back to the gypsy camp. When the old man saw her, he raised his flute. From the darkness a balalaika joined in the sweet, sad song. Anna began to dance. Pins fell from her hair and it tumbled to her shoulders. As she danced, Anna Pavlova became young again, with all the years of ballet before her. She danced and danced and danced, on and on, until the night was gone, until the music slowed and ended. The old man put down his flute as the last shivering string of the balalaika grew still. The bright sound of sleigh bells tinkled in the distance.

Anna met the young woman at the edge of the forest as she stepped down from the sleigh. The gypsy swirled the cloak from her shoulders and returned it. Without a word, she pressed the wooden heart into Anna's hand.

Anna Pavlova rode home in silence as the pale winter sun rose over the city.

Later that day, a royal messenger delivered another envelope to Anna. She sat in her ballroom before the shadowy mirrors and read: *I wish to thank you. My son, Prince Alexis, is much stronger this morning. I myself was moved by your gypsy dancing. It was as if I was seeing you for the first time on stage. The very soul of Russia danced in the room last night. May you, and my son, live forever.*

Anna Pavlova never saw the gypsies or the mysterious old woman again. Sometimes, though, when she stood alone before her mirrors, she would look at the carved wooden heart hanging about her neck. She would think for a moment of the night when she gave the gift of dance to another. Then, as the music rose, Anna Pavlova would dance again. ⬡

Czar Nicholas with his family.

AUTHOR'S NOTE

Czar Nicholas did not get his wish. Although Prince Alexis was a delicate child who suffered from a condition known as hemophilia, it wasn't his illness that killed him. In 1918, at the age of thirteen, he was assassinated with the Czar and their immediate family during the Russian Revolution.

History tells us that Anna Pavlova left Russia and did not return after 1913. If there ever was a time in her life when she feared the stage, she hid it well, for she was devoted to ballet. She established her own dance school in England and toured throughout the world performing and teaching. By 1931, when she died at age fifty, she had become an enduring symbol of her art.

Although the characters in it once lived, this story is a work of fiction. It grew out of my wondering how the lives of these people might have touched in secret ways. Who can say what mysterious and magical things happened between a ballerina, a gypsy, and a czar on a long ago, wintry, Russian night?

One thing is known. Anna Pavlova's gift was real. It has come to us down the years on the soft footsteps of every dancer, young or old, who has ever crossed a stage.

Did the story inspire you to develop your own special talent? In your notebooks, write a short personal response to the story. What was the most moving part of the story, in your opinion? Explain why.

Understanding the Story

The Gift of Dance

- Why do you think Anna Pavlova had developed a fear of dancing in public?

- What was the old gypsy woman's gift to Anna? Why did it turn out to be important to the story?

- Why did Anna ask the young gypsy woman to dance for the prince? How did Anna recover the feeling of her early dancing years at the gypsy camp?

- What does the ending of the story (the last paragraph) mean to you?

- Read the Author's Note. In your opinion, what is the most interesting difference between Maxine Trottier's story and the historical facts?

A Personal Essay

What is your gift, or special talent? Write a short personal essay about it.

Here is an outline to get you started:

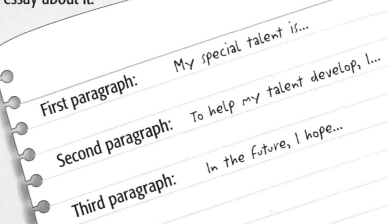

First paragraph: My special talent is...

Second paragraph: To help my talent develop, I...

Third paragraph: In the future, I hope...

Arrange a Dance Recital

IMAGINE!
Play a classical recording of a ballet such as *Swan Lake* by Tchaikovsky. As you listen, write about the pictures that come into your mind!

If you or other students in your class have studied ballet, modern dance, or jazz, arrange a short dance demonstration. Show the basic steps, typical exercises, and part of a dance that might be performed in a recital.

Find Out More About...

Ballet is famous for its female dancers, like Evelyn Hart of Winnipeg's Royal Ballet and Karen Kain and Veronica Tennant of the National Ballet of Canada. But dance fans are equally enthusiastic about male dancers. Two great Russian ballet soloists are Mikhail Baryshnikov and Rudolf Nureyev. Search your library and Internet sources to find out more about these athletic, artistic stars and the amazing physical strength they must have to perform ballet.

Frank Augustyn (left); Frank Augustyn and Veronica Tennant (middle); Karen Kain and Rudolf Nureyev (right).

Did You Know ?

To be a ballet dancer you need fitness, stamina, agility, and strength.

- Female dancers dance on the tips of their toes on pointe shoes, which puts tremendous strain on their toes, ankles, and the bones of their feet.

- Male dancers are constantly lifting their female partners, often leading to back and knee problems.

- All dancers must maintain a strict and healthy diet, and an equally strict daily exercise routine.

- Dancers begin intensive training at a very early age, and the daily wear and tear on their bodies means most of them retire before the age of forty.

Read about author Maxine Trottier on page 18.

MEET AUTHOR

Maxine Trottier

Profile by Patricia Henderson

"If you don't have any ideas for a story, don't worry about it. Hoping for inspiration is like looking for a friend—the harder you try, the worse it gets," chuckles Maxine Trottier. However, this author of more than twenty children's books has no trouble thinking up new story ideas.

"I rarely start with a plot. I start with *what if*— what if certain people came together, and what if this or that happened?

"Very early every morning, my two Yorkshire Terriers wake me up by standing on my chest. Then I head out for a brisk walk and tell myself a story from beginning to end, over and over again. I listen to music, too. The composer Chopin inspired me while I was writing *Pavlova's Gift*."

Once she has her story clear in her head, Maxine sits down at her computer and writes it. Because she also teaches grade two full time, she writes on the weekends for about three hours a day. On weekdays after school she takes care of the "business" aspect of writing—like personally answering the many letters from her young fans.

Maxine writes books for ages seven to thirteen, but the first children to hear her stories are her grade two class. "They see every step in the creation of each new story. They hear the story, see the artist's sketches, and are the first to view the finished book."

Maxine teaches her class a lot about writing and art. "Every month we have a publishing day when we publish our stories. We try to do it differently every time. Once we even shrank the text and made tiny books that we could hang around our necks. It's fun and it makes me feel good when older kids tell me that these things gave them a love of reading."

As a child, Maxine had a passion for reading. "I loved libraries because I never knew what I would find. They were so quiet and filled with possibilities.

"I was a bit like Anne of Green Gables," Maxine remembers. "I had that overactive imagination. I loved to pretend and make up names for places. That probably helped me to become a writer. After all, writing fiction is a lot like pretending."

When she was around twelve years old, Maxine wrote a lot of fairy tales about magical places—many of which took place underwater! She also loved to draw and illustrate her own stories. As an adult author, she illustrated one of her own books, called *The Big Heart*. "I really love illustrations. I wish they would put pictures into novels."

Maxine never seems to run out of new ideas. "I try to focus on the story that is sitting right in front of me. But I know the other ideas are just floating around in the background waiting for their chance to be told. If I have trouble with a story, I put it under my bed for awhile. A few weeks later I take it out and look at it with fresh eyes."

Every story Maxine writes is different, but there is one thing she tries to put in each one—a dragonfly. "Dragonflies are so beautiful," she explains. "I love their wings, their colours, and the way they move. They live most of their lives underwater, then they have one brief period in which to fly and hunt, and then they are gone." In the summer, they often land on Maxine's laptop as she writes on the deck of her sailboat.

You can see the image of the dragonfly in *Pavlova's Gift*. Find the illustration of Anna Pavlova dancing, as she often did, in a winged costume.

Maxine loves her work and "wants to write endlessly" from her home in Port Stanley, Ontario. Her latest book, *The Walking Stick*, is about the war in Vietnam. She highly recommends it for grade six students.

To young authors who love to bring a story to life, Maxine offers these words of wisdom: "To be a writer, you have to be a reader. Good readers are good writers. You have to read and write every day and write with joy. I do."

When you look in a mirror, is that you? Or is there part of yourself that the mirror can't reveal? Read on to discover how artist George Littlechild tried to reveal his true self through his painting.

George Littlechild
is a painter, printmaker, and mixed-media artist whose works are exhibited in galleries and museums throughout the world. A member of the Plains Cree Nation of Canada, he was born in Edmonton, Alberta, in 1958 and now lives in Vancouver, British Columbia.

Self-Portrait

**Autobiography and Artwork
by George Littlechild**

When I was a boy, people knew I was Indian (or First Nations, as we say in Canada) because I had the features of my Indian mother. As I got older, people weren't sure anymore. "You sure are exotic-looking," they told me. "Are you Spanish? Italian? Portuguese?" I was looking more like my white father. But since both my parents were dead and I was living with my Dutch foster family, I was very confused about who I was. No one ever told me then that I was mixed-blood.

Sometimes I look Indian now, but sometimes I don't. My looks change according to my mood. That's why I've made these four different self-portraits. It took me many years to accept my features. Then one day I decided that I had to love myself just the way I am. I'm a rainbow man, with a half of this and a quarter of that, and a dash of a mixture of everything! ◆

FOLLOW UP

If you were painting your own self-portrait, how many portraits would you make? Why?

Understanding the Selection

Rainbow Man

- Why was George Littlechild confused about his identity while he was growing up?

- Why did he choose to make four different self-portraits? Do you think this was a good solution?

- How did the phrase "rainbow man" help George to accept himself just the way he is?

The Creative Arts

MAKE A WEB

Reread the poem *I am the creativity* on page 7. In a small group or as a class, discuss the following questions.

- What does "creativity" mean to you? What does it mean to poet Alexis De Veaux?

- What do you think Alexis means by "I am the creativity/keeping my people/alive"?

- Do you think George Littlechild would agree with this idea? Explain your answer.

Make a web with the word **Creativity** in the centre. Around it, put all the arts mentioned in the poem. What are some of the special arts of various Canadian cultural groups? Add them to your Creativity Web. What else can you add to this web?

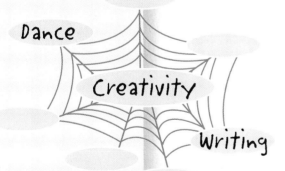

Dance

Creativity

Writing

Viewing Self-Portraits

Look at George's four self-portraits in detail. In what ways are they similar and different? How do they compare with his photograph on page 20? What is the effect of the colours he chooses? What details of his clothing are most striking? How does he reveal his mixed ancestry in his portraits? Now compare George's self-portraits to these self-portraits by other artists.

Vincent Van Gogh

Joyce Weiland

Malvin Gray Johnson

Make Your Own Self-Portrait

Home Link

There are many ways to create your own self-portrait. If you like to paint, use oils or watercolour. You can also draw and colour with crayons, pastel chalks, charcoal, or just pencil. Or, if you prefer, make a collage using photos and favourite objects that represent you. Begin by looking in the mirror at different times. Decide how you want to look in your portrait. Then just do it—and be creative! Share your portrait with family members or classmates, explaining what you've done.

 TECH LINK

If you have access to multimedia software, use images and sound to create your portrait.

IMAGINE!

What if George Littlechild or one of these other artists was a character in a story? What's behind the self-portrait? You write the story!

◆

If you could play
your favourite
fictional character
on TV, who would
you choose?
Martha MacIsaac
was lucky enough
to play a character
from her home
province, Prince
Edward Island!

A R T I C L E
F R O M
*K I D S W O R L D
M A G A Z I N E*

Emily of New Moon

Emily of New Moon: The TV Series

Emily of New Moon is an action-packed Canadian television series. Each episode covers another adventure in the life of Emily, a girl who lived on Prince Edward Island almost 100 years ago. The series is based on books by L.M. Montgomery, the much-loved author of *Anne of Green Gables*.

After the death of her mother and father, Emily is forced to live with strict relatives at the family farm called New Moon. Emily experiences many hardships, but her tremendous zest for life helps her to overcome them.

Curiosity and the dream of becoming a great writer lead Emily on many adventures. In the first series of shows, she runs away from New Moon, writes in secret, gets trapped in a house by spirits, assists in delivering a baby, and witnesses a public hanging!

Meet Martha, Star of *New Moon*

Eighty kids from across Canada auditioned for the part of Emily in the TV series *Emily of New Moon*. In the end, the producers chose Martha MacIsaac, a thirteen-year-old student at Queen Charlotte Junior High School in Charlottetown, Prince Edward Island. We asked Martha to tell us about life as a celebrity.

Q How were you chosen to act the part of Emily?

Martha Marlene Matthews (the senior producer of the show) came to Prince Edward Island looking for a little girl to play Emily. Someone mentioned my name and I met her. Then I had a couple of auditions on the Island. After that I went to Toronto for the final audition, and I got the part.

Q What do kids have to do when they go to an audition for a show like *Emily of New Moon*?

Martha They give you a couple of pages of the script to learn, and then you go in and read it for the casting director.

Q How does it feel to be a special kid on the set, and then have to go home and just be one of the family?

Emily's chores include collecting seaweed to be placed at the base of the house for insulation.

Martha No one treats me extra special here, so it's not that difficult.

Q Emily has a very hard life compared to lots of kids in Canada today. How do you think she manages to overcome all the horrible things that happen to her?

Martha She escapes into her imagination, sometimes.

Q When you have to cry as Emily, are you really crying, or do they put fake tears on your face?

Martha Not usually. If they need to have fake tears they blow crystals in my eyes.

Q What do you do about school when you are acting?

Martha My tutor, Elaine Strawbridge, teaches me and all the other kids on set between shots.

Q How does it differ from real school?

Martha It's different because we only go to school for short periods of time and there's not very many kids in the class. I get to work with the tutor by myself a lot.

Q Tell us about the newsletter that the kids put together.

Martha Every episode, all of the kids from *Emily* write articles about what's going on at the show and in the world. There are interviews with famous people, gossip columns, and many other things.

Q Is there anything else you think readers would find interesting about your experiences?

Martha I get to work with some of the best Canadian talent, and it's fun!

Emily and her friends discover a chicken killed by a raccoon.

Who Is Lucy Maud Montgomery?

The *Emily of New Moon* television series is based on the story *Emily of New Moon* written by Lucy Maud Montgomery. Maud, as she liked to be called, wrote two more books about Emily's life: *Emily Climbs* and *Emily's Quest*. Maud is best known for writing *Anne of Green Gables* and seven more novels about Anne and her family. Born in 1873, she started writing the *Anne* series of books in 1903, while living on Prince Edward Island. Although the *Anne* and *Emily* books take place on Prince Edward Island, Maud moved to Ontario in 1911, where she began writing the *Emily* books in 1923.

Anne of Green Gables has been translated into seventeen different languages and is read by children and adults around the world. It has also been made into a popular TV movie and a musical performed in Charlottetown every summer.

Many people come from other countries to visit Prince Edward Island because they like the *Anne* stories so much and want to see first-hand the land and the sea described in the books.

Maud wrote twenty-five books, more than 500 short stories, and many poems. When she was nine years old, she started writing a diary. Maud kept writing journals throughout her life. Many are now in print, so everyone can read them.

Anne of Green Gables is Maud's most popular character, but from her journals we discover that the *Emily* stories are more like Maud's own life.

A Kid's Life 100 Years Ago

Chores, Chores, and More Chores

Children had to work before school and after school. They did everything: milking the cows, pumping water (there were no taps), storing food in the cellar for winter, spinning, knitting, and much more.

Long Walks to School

Although all children were required to go to school, those in farming areas often missed class to help their parents on the farm. One-room schoolhouses were the norm on Prince Edward Island, and children usually walked for long distances to get there. Because they had no food for lunch, the teacher would boil up a pot of oatmeal for the hungry students.

Cold Trips to the Washroom

All toilets were outdoors. And forget outdoor lighting! They didn't even have electric lights inside. Most homes had gas lamps, but at New Moon, Emily's stern Aunt Elizabeth would only allow candles.

Did Kids Have Any Fun?

Yes, despite all those chores, long walks to school, and severe punishment, children enjoyed many of the things you enjoy today. They liked to fish, play games in the woods, do arts and crafts (using fish bones, twigs, and stones) and put on plays and concerts.

Emily and her best friend, Ilse, share fun times and sad times.

Would you like to have the opportunity that Martha had? What do you think would be the most fun about acting in a television series?

Understanding the Article

From Maud to Martha

- Why do you think the producers thought *Emily of New Moon* would make a good TV series?

- Apart from her acting talent, why is it fitting that Martha MacIsaac was selected to play the part of Emily?

- In the interview, Martha says,"No one treats me extra special here." Do you think that's surprising? What questions would you like to ask her?

- Have you read L.M. Montgomery's most famous book, *Anne of Green Gables*, or seen the movie? Why do you think Anne is so popular?

- Do you enjoy stories set in the past—100 years ago or more? Why do we still enjoy such stories today?

IMAGINE!

You've been asked to create a TV series based on your favourite Canadian novel! Choose the book, then outline the first three episodes.

Media Link Family TV Shows

What TV shows does your family like to watch together? How would you describe a good family show? How does it appeal to old and young alike?

Interview a Performer

Do you have a friend, acquaintance, or family member who is a performer–a musician, actor, dancer, or athlete? Make a list of ten questions you would like to ask that person. When you interview him or her, make notes or use a tape recorder. When you write up the interview, follow the question-and-answer model in this selection.

TIP You will probably need to "clean up" the answers to make the interview readable. Most people say "umm" and "let me see" and "you know" quite often!

A TV Drama Review

Watch and review an episode of *Emily of New Moon* or another current Canadian TV drama series for young people. Does it rate

★ poor
★★ fair
★★★ good
★★★★ excellent?

First, fill in a chart like this one in your notebook.

TV Drama Review

Elements	Poor	Fair	Good	Excellent
Casting: choice of actors for each part				
Acting: how well the actors perform				
Location: buildings, streets, scenery, etc.				
Camera work: lighting, camera angles, etc.				
Story line: fast or slow pace, suspense, emotional content				
Dialogue: the words the characters say				
Tone: humorous, dark, exciting				

Something To Think About

The character Emily in *Emily of New Moon* lived almost 100 years ago. Would you have enjoyed living back then? How would your life be different? the same?

Now, turn your notes into paragraphs to write your review. Choose a good opening sentence to hook your readers. Describe the show—without giving away the best parts! Give your opinions of the various elements of the show.

Compare it to your favourite show. Conclude with a summary of your opinions and a one- to four-star rating.

Music to My Ears

The Conductor's Hands

See the magic music glisten
     in his quick magician's hands;
music flickers in his fingers,
     watch him weave it into strands
of sound he wraps around you
     from your ankles to your hair;
mesmerized by silver sound, you
     watch him pluck the notes from air.

Alice Schertle

Taking Violin at School

I open my case
tighten my bow
pluck a string to tune.
I love to listen to it chirp across the echoing room.

My friends are in class
reading about
a famous English king,
But I am training this wooden bird upon my arm to sing.

April Halprin Wayland

Music Class

I hear birds. I sing frogs.
My heart hears every note,
Yet my song is locked
Inside my throat.
Someone laughs,
I'm way off-key.

The teacher holds my hand
And opens a special box
Of things with secret voices.

I get maracas and triangle.
I am aria. I am madrigal.
With silver bells and tambourine
        I can sing!

Kristine O'Connell George

No Static

dialing down the stations
tune in hot-shot rock
a compact sound companion
everywhere I walk

the beat gets in my blood
pounding down the street
plugged into my head
the music fuels my feet

walking with my radio
the city noises gone
the place between my ears
wall-to-wall song

Monica Kulling

Personal Response

- Do you like to sing, to play a musical instrument, or both? What is your favourite instrument?
- What does April Wayland like best about playing her violin? How do you think beginners sound when they play the violin?
- What is in the special box in Kristine George's poem? How do the contents of the box help her to sing?
- What is magical about the conductor's hands in Alice Schertle's poem? Would you like to try conducting?
- What music do you think Monica Kulling is listening to as she walks down the street?
- What music do you like to listen to?

A Poem

Surveys show that nearly everybody loves music. What is your favourite kind of music? Think about a special musical experience you have had—attending a concert, taking part in a school performance, forming your own band, or hearing music in an unexpected place. Write a poem about your experience. Use one of the poems in *Music to My Ears* as a model, if you wish.

Create a Live Sound Track

Create a live sound track to accompany a show (such as a video, slide show, poetry reading, or anything you like). Work with a small group of students who sing or play a variety of instruments. Select music to fit the mood and pace of the show you are accompanying. Each student should have a few minutes to play or sing. Make sure the music flows smoothly from one voice or instrument to the next. Finally, time the whole sound track so that it fits exactly with the work you are accompanying.

POET'S CRAFT
Metaphors in Verbs

How do you describe the sound of music? In *The Conductor's Hands*, Alice Schertle uses unusual verbs to suggest comparisons to the sounds of music: "glisten" (suggests shiny metal), "flickers" (suggests flames), "weave" and "wraps" (suggest fabric). Find out what some of the following instruments sound like. Invent verbs that suggest comparisons to these sounds.

- a steel drum
- a wild Celtic fiddle
- an Indian sitar
- a Japanese koto
- a tiny piccolo
- an electric guitar
- South American panpipes
- your choice of instrument or voice

IMAGINE!

You're organizing a concert. Your classmates are presenting all sorts of music—from blues to bells to birdsong. Make a poster inviting one and all!

Musical Terms

aria: a solo song with a soaring melody, often from an opera

madrigal: a song from the Renaissance (500 years ago) in four- or five-part harmony; often has a "fa la la" chorus

maracas: a pair of percussion instruments that look and sound like rattles

tambourine: a shallow drum with jingling metal disks around the side

triangle: a metal triangle that "pings" when hit with a stick

violin: a stringed instrument held under the chin and played with a bow

Listen to...the Instruments of the Orchestra

Locate and play a recording of Benjamin Britten's *A Young Person's Guide to the Orchestra*. This famous piece introduces each instrument of the orchestra separately so you can hear how it sounds, alone and in combination with other instruments.

Susan Aglukark wanted to be a singer when she grew up. But she didn't think it would ever be possible for a girl living in the Far North. This is a portrait of how she overcame obstacles and achieved her dream.

PROFILE BY
Monica Kulling

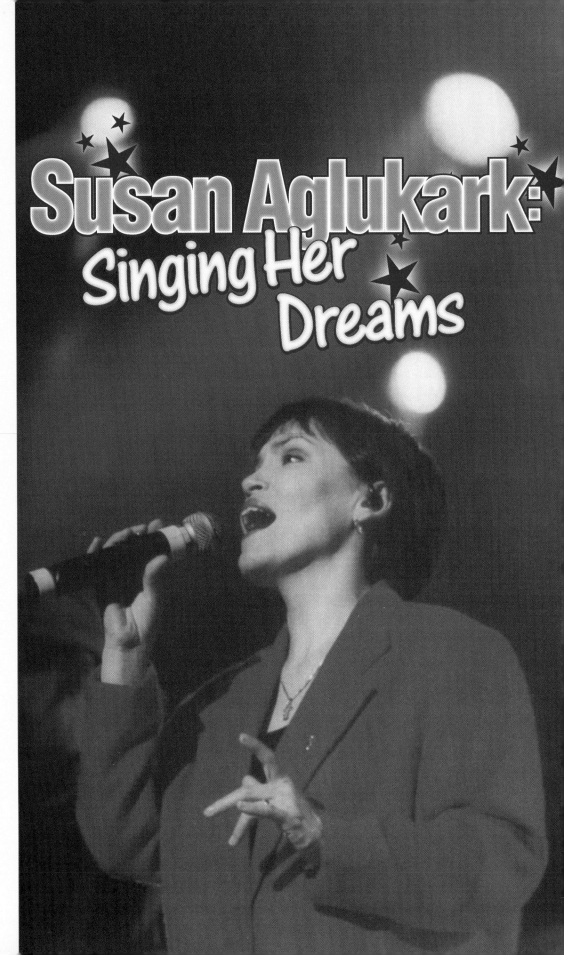

Susan Aglukark:
Singing Her Dreams

Susan Aglukark is speaking to a group of Inuit students. The singer tells her young audience to be proud of their Inuit culture and tradition. Her brown eyes dance with delight as she speaks of her love for the North, of her passion for the traditional ways of her people.

Susan's songs bridge the distance between the old and the new. She sings about the past, but she also tackles the big issues facing the young Inuit of today. The song "O Siem," from her third CD, *This Child*, is typical of the messages that Susan's songs carry.

As Susan explains, "A line in the song, *'siem o siyeya,'* means all peoples, all cultures and races, all people rich and poor. The song talks about watching the walls come tumbling down, and by that I mean the walls of racism and prejudice, of hate and anger."

Susan Aglukark is an Inuk (member of the Inuit). She was born in Churchill, Manitoba, in 1967. For the first twelve years of her life, Susan's family moved around Nunavut quite a bit. Finally, they settled in Arviat, a small community on the western shore of Hudson Bay, about 1400 km north of Winnipeg. It was here that Susan began singing. Her father was a minister and she sang in the church choir.

Susan grew up wanting to be a pilot or a recording artist. But such dreams seemed out of reach for a girl growing up in the Far North. In her teens, Susan began playing the guitar and writing her own songs. In one of her first songs, "Dreams for You," Susan reminds her father about the dreams she had when she was younger:

> "I was told I was a dreamer
> wanting things I couldn't have
> And Daddy here I am
> Singing my song
> Singing my dreams for you."

Susan went to high school in the city of Yellowknife because there were no high schools near her home. After school, she moved to Ottawa, Ontario. She worked as a translator for the Department of Indian Affairs and Northern Development, as well as for the Inuit Tapirisat of Canada*. Susan liked her work. It was satisfying representing her people. It was fun working in the language she grew up speaking, which is Inuktitut. But Susan still had her dreams. She still wanted to be a singer.

With the help of CBC Radio, Susan released a cassette of gospel songs. It was a beginning, but Susan had even bigger dreams. One day she asked her friend Val Haas if she would be her manager. Val had trained as a social worker. She didn't know anything about the music industry. But it sounded exciting and Val was willing to learn. The two women left Ottawa. They invested their money in Susan's second recording, *Arctic Rose*.

Susan's music career really took off when talent scouts from a major recording label heard this album. They signed Susan to a six-album contract. Her third album, *This Child*, was released in 1995. It has sold many thousands of copies. There are songs on this album written in English, but there are also songs written in Inuktitut. Haunting drums and the whistling Arctic wind can be heard on several of the songs.

Susan performs with First Nations children in High River, Alberta, August 1995.

---

* **Inuit Tapirisat of Canada:** an organization that represents all the Inuit regions of Canada. Its goals are to preserve Inuit language and culture, and to speak up for Inuit needs and interests.

Susan sings about what it's like to live in the North. The vast landscape of the Arctic is a presence in her music. In a song called "Hina Na Ho" Susan sings of surviving winter.

"The song tells of surviving another winter. But it isn't only the season we've survived, it is also our own personal battles. The song also talks about the Creator, because aboriginal people have great respect for the creator of the land."

Susan Aglukark stepped into the spotlight only a few short years ago. In that time, she's accomplished many things. She has appeared on television shows and she's been written about in many magazines. She's performed in her home town. She's won many awards, including the first ever Aboriginal Achievement Award in 1994. Susan continues to write songs and will soon release her fourth CD.

Susan keeps a busy performing and speaking schedule. It is her desire to help the young Inuit of today by setting an example. She urges them to stay in school, to stay away from drugs, and to dream their dreams. Susan isn't singing just for herself and she knows it.

"There's so much resting on my shoulders as a role model," admits Susan. "I'm setting a way for my people."

And she is doing a fine job. Susan Aglukark has proven that it is possible to dream big dreams and to see those dreams come true.

My Hero, Susan Aglukark

Shawna Tatty
Grade 9,
Maani Ulujuk Ilinniarvik School
Rankin Inlet, Nunavut

Susan Aglukark is a very kind-hearted person, and everyone knows that. You can tell by listening to her beautiful voice, and by that smile on her face.

Susan's first video was *Searching*. The video shots were done in Ottawa and the northern shots were done in Arviat. I found it the best music video, and that's when I knew that she was my hero. An Inuk who is able to have that kind of talent and show us what she's feeling is so important.

Susan tells young people that we don't have to give up easily on things we have started. I was about to give up on this project I'm working on until I read Susan's words in one of the magazine stories about her. She encouraged me to work harder instead of giving up.

I am proud of Susan. She is a very good example to our people.

FOLLOW UP

What do you think was the most important thing Susan did to make her dreams come true? Why is Susan a hero to student Shawna Tatty?

YOUR TURN TO WRITE

My Hero...

Susan Aglukark feels that she is a "role model" for her people. What does this phrase mean to you? Who do you look up to as a role model? Why? Write a short personal essay with three or four paragraphs, like the one by Shawna Tatty. Call it **My Hero** …

1st paragraph: Describe your hero and what the person does.

2nd paragraph: Give reasons why you admire your hero.

3rd paragraph: Explain the message the person has given you.

Understanding the Article

Singing My Dreams

- What steps did Susan take on her way to becoming a singer?
- Who helped Susan to get her songs heard and become known in Canada?
- What kinds of issues does Susan tackle in her songs?
- If you were to listen to one of Susan's albums, what sounds would tell you that her songs are about life in the Far North?
- Why do you think Susan writes her songs in both English and Inuktitut?
- What messages does Susan have for young Inuit when she speaks to them? Do you think all young people should listen to her ideas?

Listening...

Listen to one of Susan Aglukark's recordings, such as *Arctic Rose* or *This Child*. In your notebook, try to describe her music. What singers would you compare her to? Listen carefully to the words as well. What lines in her songs impress you the most? Watch for Susan in music videos, too.

Find Out More About...

Susan wants Inuit young people to be proud of their culture and traditions. But she knows that the traditional Inuit way of life is changing, and that big changes are always difficult. Search your library and the Internet for more information about the traditional way of life and how it is changing today.

IMAGINE!
You have won a plane ticket to Susan's home town of Arviat and she's giving a concert! What will you see, hear, and experience there?

Change for the Better

SMALL GROUP DISCUSSION

In some of her songs, Susan Aglukark has a message—she wants to bring about change for the better. For example, in her song "O Siem," she talks about tumbling the "walls of racism and prejudice, of hate and anger." In a small group, make a list of popular songs that have a message. Discuss why songs can be a powerful way to make a message widely known, and to change people's minds.

The Jade Stone

A Chinese folk tale, adapted by
Caryn Yacowitz

Illustrations by
Harvey Chan

11+ Roles: Narrator 1, Narrator 2, Narrator 3, Narrator 4, Chan Lo, Emperor, Stone, Adviser 1, Adviser 2, Adviser 3, Apprentice, Emperor's Guards

Narrator 1: Long ago in China there lived a stone carver named

Chan Lo: *(bowing)* Chan Lo.

Narrator 4: Chan Lo spent his days carving birds and deer and water buffalo from the coloured stones he found near the river.

Narrator 2: His young apprentice asked,

Apprentice: How do you know what to carve?

Chan Lo: I always listen to the stone.

Narrator 3: ...replied Chan Lo.

Chan Lo: The stone tells me what it wants to be.

Narrator 1: People came from near and far to buy Chan Lo's carvings.

Narrator 4: So it happened that when the Great Emperor of All China was given a perfect piece of green-and-white jade stone, one of the advisers in the Celestial Palace thought of

Adviser 1: Chan Lo!

Narrator 2: The humble stone carver was brought before the Great Emperor of All China. Chan Lo bowed deeply.

Emperor: I want you to carve a dragon.

Narrator 3: ...the emperor commanded.

Emperor: A dragon of wind and fire.

Chan Lo: I will do my best to please you.

Narrator 1: The emperor's men carried the precious stone to Chan Lo's garden.

Narrator 4: Chan Lo had never seen such a perfect piece of jade. The green-and-white of the stone was like moss-entangled-in-snow.

Narrator 2: The great emperor had commanded "a dragon of wind and fire." Chan Lo wondered if that was what the stone wanted to be. He spoke to it.

Chan Lo: Here I stand, O Noble Stone,
to carve a creature of your own.
Whisper signs and sounds from rock
that I, your servant, may unlock.

Narrator 3: Chan Lo bent down and put his ear to the stone. From deep inside came a gentle sound.

Stone: *(softly)* Pah-tah. Pah-tah. Pah-tah.

Chan Lo: Do dragons make that sound?

Narrator 1: ...Chan Lo wondered.

Chan Lo: Perhaps the dragon's tail splashing in the ocean says "Pah-tah, pah-tah."

Narrator 4: But he was not sure.

Narrator 2: That evening, Chan Lo thought about dragons.

Narrator 3: But late at night, in his dreams, he heard,

Stone: Pah-tah. Pah-tah.

Stone & Chan Lo: *Pah-tah.*

Narrator 1: The next morning, Chan Lo went to the garden.

Narrator 4: The stone was spring-water-green in the morning light.

Chan Lo: Here I stand, O Noble Stone, to carve a creature of your own. Whisper signs and sounds from rock that I, your servant, may unlock.

Narrator 2: Chan Lo put his ear to the green-and-white jade and listened.

Narrator 3: Softly the sounds came.

Stone: *(softly)* Bub-bub-bubble. Bub-bub-bubble.

Chan Lo: Do dragons make that sound?

Narrator 1: ...Chan Lo asked himself.

Chan Lo: Perhaps a dragon rising from the wild waves blows bubbles through his nostrils.

Narrator 4: But these were not mighty dragon bubbles that were coming from the rock. They were gentle, lazy, playful sounds.

Narrator 2: That evening, Chan Lo tried again to think about dragons.

Narrator 3: But when he went to bed, he heard in his dreams the sound of

Stone: Bub-bub-bubble. Bub-bub-bubble.

Stone & Chan Lo: Bub-bub-bubble.

Narrator 1: In the middle of the night, Chan Lo awoke. He walked into the moonlit garden.

Narrator 4: The stone shone silvery-green in the moonlight.

Chan Lo: Here I stand, O Noble Stone, to carve a creature of your own. Whisper signs and sounds from rock that I, your servant, may unlock.

Narrator 2: He put his ear to the stone. Silence.

Narrator 3: Chan Lo ran his hands over the jade.
His fingers felt tiny ridges, and the ridges made a sound.

Stone: *(softly)* S-s-s-ah, S-s-s-s-ah, S-s-s-s-s-s-ah.

Chan Lo: Do dragons have ridges?

Narrator 1: ...Chan Lo pondered.

Chan Lo: Yes. They have scales. Scales on their tails and bodies.
And their scales might say, "S-s-s-ah, S-s-s-s-ah, S-s-s-s-s-s-ah,"
if one dared to touch them.

Narrator 4: But Chan Lo knew these small, delicate ridges were
not dragon scales.

Narrator 2: Chan Lo could not carve what he did not hear, but
he was afraid to disobey the emperor.

Narrator 3: His fear weighed in him like a great stone as he
picked up his tools and began to carve.

* * *

Narrator 1: Chan Lo worked slowly and carefully for a year
and a day.

Narrator 4: Finally, the carving was complete.

Narrator 2: Early in the morning, before the birds were awake,
Chan Lo and his apprentice wrapped the jade carving in a
cloth and set out for the Celestial Palace.

Narrator 3: Chan Lo entered the Great Hall, where the three
advisers sat waiting for the Great Emperor of All China. He
placed the jade stone on the table in the centre of the room.

Narrator 1: Soon the emperor's advisers grew curious. They
scurried to the jade stone and peeked under the cloth.

Adviser 1: *(surprised)* No dragon!

Adviser 2: *(louder)* No dragon!

Adviser 3: *(loudest)* NO DRAGON!

Narrator 4: At that moment, the emperor himself entered the Great Hall.

Emperor: Show me my dragon of wind and fire!

Narrator 2: The advisers whisked the cloth away.

Emperor: *(thundering)* This is not my dragon!

Adviser 1: *(pointing at Chan Lo)* Punish him!

Adviser 2: *Punish him!*

Adviser 3: PUNISH HIM!

Narrator 3: Chan Lo's knees shook like ginkgo leaves in the wind.

Chan Lo: O mighty emperor, there is no dragon of wind and fire. I did not *hear* it! I heard these three carp fish swimming playfully in the reeds in the pool of the Celestial Palace.

Emperor: *Hear* them? You did not *hear* them!

Narrator 1: The emperor was so angry, he could not decide which punishment to choose.

Emperor: I will let my *dreams* decide his punishment. Now, take him away! And remove that stone from the Celestial Palace!

Narrator 4: Chan Lo was dragged down many flights of stairs and thrown into a black prison cell. The carving was placed outside, near the reeds of the reflecting pool.

* * *

Narrator 2: That evening, the emperor thought about dragons.

Narrator 3: But late that night, in his sleep, the emperor dreamed of fish playfully slapping their tails in green water.

Stone: Pah-tah. Pah-tah.

Stone & Emperor: Pah-*tah*.

Narrator 1: In the morning, the emperor's advisers asked,

Adviser 1: What punishment have you chosen?

Narrator 4: But the emperor said,

Emperor: My dreams have not yet decided.

Narrator 2: That evening, the emperor again tried to think about dragons.

Narrator 3: But when he went to bed, the emperor dreamed of fish gliding smoothly through deep, clear water.

Stone: Bub-bub-bubble. Bub-bub-bubble.

Stone & Emperor: Bub-bub-bubble.

Narrator 1: In the morning, the emperor's advisers again asked him,

Adviser 2: What punishment have your dreams chosen?

Narrator 4: But the emperor told them,

Emperor: My dreams have still not decided.

Narrator 2: On the third night, the emperor groaned and tossed in his sleep, but he did not dream.

Narrator 3: He awoke in the darkest hour of the night. A strange sound filled the room.

Stone: S-s-s-ah, S-s-s-s-s-ah, S-s-s-s-s-s-s-ah.

Narrator 1: The emperor got out of bed and went toward the sound. He hurried down the corridors, through the Great Hall, and out into the moonlit garden.

Narrator 4: There by the reflecting pool was the jade stone. Next to it stood the apprentice, running his fingers down the scales of the three carp fish.

Stone: S-s-s-ah, S-s-s-s-s-ah, S-s-s-s-s-s-s-ah.

Narrator 2: When the apprentice had gone, the emperor sat near the pool and gazed at the jade stone. The shining scales of the jade carp glowed in the moonlight. The fishes' slippery bodies were reflected in the pool. They seemed ready to flick their tails and swim among the reeds.

Narrator 3: The emperor remained by the pool until his advisers found him at sunrise.

Adviser 3: What punishment have your dreams chosen?

Emperor: *(smiling)* Bring Chan Lo before me.

* * *

Narrator 1: Chan Lo bowed deeply before the Great Emperor of All China, ready to receive his terrible punishment.

Emperor: You have disobeyed me, Chan Lo, but you are a brave man to defy the Great Emperor of All China. You have carved the creatures that were in the stone. I, too, have heard them. These three carp fish are dearer to me than any dragon of wind and fire. What reward would you have?

Chan Lo: *(grateful and relieved, bowing even lower)* Great Emperor, your happiness with my work is my reward. I wish only to return to my village and carve what I hear.

Emperor: You *will* carve what you hear. And you will return to your village in great honour—as befits the Master Carver to the Great Emperor of All China!

Stone: Pah-*tah!*

RESPONDING

FOLLOW
UP

How did Chan Lo
get out of his
predicament? Did
you find the ending
of the folk tale
satisfying?

Understanding the Selection

- How does Chan Lo decide what he is going to carve? Why is this method so important to him?
- What does the Emperor command Chan Lo to carve from the perfect jade stone?
- What happens when Chan Lo listens to the jade stone? Why is he fearful when he begins to carve it?
- What do you think Chan Lo expects to happen when he carries his carving to the Celestial Palace?
- At what moment in the tale is Chan Lo saved from punishment by the Emperor?
- In your opinion, what is the message of this folk tale?

IMAGINE!

The Emperor has commanded you to step into the spotlight and share your special talent! What will you do for your command performance?

Creativity

CLASS DISCUSSION

Chan Lo, the stone carver, says that his greatest happiness is to "carve what I hear." This is one way to describe the creative process. Some Inuit sculptors use similar language to describe how they carve.

Do you think "listening" can be applied to other arts? Do composers listen before they write music? Do painters listen to the canvas? Do actors listen before they speak? What about writers? What other words could you use to describe how you (and other artists) tap into your creative sources?

48 INTO THE SPOTLIGHT

Act It Out

Work with eleven or more students to prepare a dramatic reading of *The Jade Stone*. The director's notes offer hints and suggestions for your performance. Enjoy!

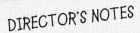

DIRECTOR'S NOTES

ACTORS

FOUR NARRATORS: You people are very important to the story. Read as clearly and expressively as you can. Stand or sit a little apart from the main action. Use gestures to indicate each character as he or she enters.

CHAN LO: You are quiet, but competent and sure of your talent.

APPRENTICE: You are humble and loyal to your master.

EMPEROR: You are lordly and overbearing, but don't need to shout.

THREE ADVISERS: You are inclined to be mean and conceited. You need to decide what makes each of you a little different from the other two.

STONE: You have a wonderful part! As you make your gentle sounds, think of yourself as a fish in a pond!

EMPEROR'S MEN and GUARDS: You have your choice as to how many of you there are and what you do in the performance.

MOVEMENTS

The narrators often tell the audience what is happening. But you actors need to do what the narrators say as well. Narrators, allow plenty of time for the actors to move about. For example:
- The Emperor's men lead Chan Lo to the Palace to see the Emperor.
- Both Chan Lo and the Emperor lie down to sleep & dream three times.

Look for other examples of movements as you rehearse your dramatic reading.

COSTUMES, PROPS, AND LIGHTING

COSTUMES: optional. Check the story illustrations for ideas.

PROPS: Decide if you need to show Chan Lo's carving or not. You could just bring the cloth covering and let the palace folk (and the audience) imagine what they see underneath.

LIGHTING: Even in the classroom, someone can turn the lights on and off to indicate day and night.

AUDIENCE

Listen carefully, enjoy, and applaud! The performance is for you!

Big Words, Strong Words: Martin Luther King, Jr.

Poem by Bobbi Katz

They called him M.L.,
the little boy who rough-housed with his brother
who sat between his mother
and his grandmother on Sunday mornings,
listening to his father's sermons.
He listened more to the rhythm
of the words
than to the words themselves—
words he did not always understand.
He felt the grown-ups around him
carried by the words—
the way the current carried branches
and even trees
down the stream.
He saw the strength of words—their power.
"Someday," he told his mother,
"I'm going to get me some words—
big words, strong words."

And he did.

Personal Response

- Have you ever heard someone speak in a way that impressed you? Share your memories with others in your group.
- What do you think poet Bobbi Katz means in these lines: "He listened more to the rhythm of the words than to the words themselves"?
- If you had "big words, strong words," what would you tell the world?

Big Words, Strong Words

"I have a dream today...that one day right there in Alabama, little black boys and black girls will be able to join hands with little white boys and white girls as sisters and brothers. I have a dream today!"

(words spoken by Martin Luther King, Jr. at the March on Washington, August 1963)

MORE GOOD READING

❦ **Tchaikovsky Discovers America**
by Esther Kalman
Eleven-year-old Jenny Petroff meets the great musician Peter Ilich Tchaikovsky, the composer of the famous ballet *Swan Lake*, on his only visit to America in 1891. This touching story is told through Jenny's diary entries. (a picture book)

Just Like Me: Stories and Self-Portraits by Fourteen Artists
George Littlechild is just one of the artists featured in this colourful collection. Through stories, paintings, and childhood photos, artists from Canada, the United States, and Mexico share what inspired them to become artists for children. (autobiographies)

❦ *Emily of New Moon*
by L.M. Montgomery
Meet Emily as she first appeared on the pages of L.M. Montgomery's book. Read how writing in her beloved journal helped her to deal with her parents' deaths, her new surroundings, and her new friends. (a novel)

Martin Luther King, Jr.
by Diane Patrick
Martin Luther King, Jr. lived for only thirty-nine years, but in his short lifetime he helped to change the way black Americans were treated. He was a remarkable writer and a powerful speaker. This fascinating book explains how he gained the wisdom and the courage he needed to achieve his goals. (a biography)

Summer Vacation

Poem by **Beverley Brenna**

Illustration by **Jimminy Roux**

This year, try something new.
Space Travel offers a deal you can't refuse.
Eight days and nights
that are out of this world.
Challenging.
Refreshing.
This year,
spend your vacation on the moon!
Tour the Sea of Dreams.
　　— Where else can you practise your air stroke,
　　　lunar crawl, and flutter jump?
Climb craters,
Dance to moon rock.
Leave your troubles below you.
For a lighthearted holiday,
book early to avoid disappointment.
Regular price for full moon,
reductions for quarters.

Personal Response

- What sports are described in the poem? Why can't they be played on earth? Do you think you would enjoy playing these sports?
- Do you think people will ever really take vacations on the moon? What activity would be the most fun?

Advertising Messages

Media Link

Summer Vacation is a poem that sounds a lot like an advertisement. What words make it sound that way? With your classmates, discuss the poem and its tone. Does the poem convince you that a summer vacation on the moon would be terrific? What are some common phrases advertisers use to convince people to buy things?

Write your own advertising poem persuading readers they should book one of the following vacations:

- a cruise on a submarine
- a hike to a volcano
- a golf game with a gorilla
- your choice

Design a Future Travel Brochure

Where would you like to travel twenty-five years from now? Think about how travel might be different in the future—new destinations, new ways of getting there, and new vacation activities. You might travel in space, visit an underground city, or explore below the earth's surface. Pick your favourite future vacation spot and design a travel brochure for it. You'll need:

- a title and an attractive picture for the cover
- details about transportation
- an itinerary (a schedule of what people will do each day)
- a description of the food and accommodation
- a price list for first-class and economy customers

IMAGINE!
You've just got home from your vacation on the moon. Write an e-mail letter to your travel agent telling her just what you thought of the trip.

Performing the Poem

Home Link

Prepare a presentation of this poem for family members or classmates. Begin by reading the poem to yourself several times, thinking about its meaning and mood. As you rehearse, remember to experiment with volume, speed, and expression. Record your reading on a tape recorder and listen to it. When you're satisfied with your reading, present the poem to an audience.

WRITER'S CRAFT

Humour

What makes this poem funny? It's a tough question because everyone has a unique sense of humour. But poet Beverley Brenna uses some good techniques to get readers smiling. Here are a couple to discuss with three or four classmates:

- double meaning: "out of this world"
- puns: "dance to moon rock"

Find more funny lines in the poem and talk about what makes them funny. What's the joke in the last two lines? Why do both poets and advertisers use humour?

Responding Activities **55**

BEFORE READING

◆

Imagine what life will be like when you're a grandparent! That's what writer Catherine Rondina has done. The "news" in her Internet newspaper comes from her fertile imagination. Read on to get some idea of how you might be living in the future.

Newspaper by
Catherine Rondina

Illustrations by
Steve Attoe

Globe Star

Saturday, April 1, 2060   **Circulation: 570 000 000**   **Price: $5.00**

GLOBAL NEWS

Greenland Joins Confederation

by SAMI PETROVAS-KWOK

Yesterday, Greenland residents voted ninety-eight percent in favour of joining the Global Confederation. As early as 2061, Greenland will become Section 250. Recent economic problems convinced Greenlanders of the benefits of becoming members. "We're tired of living on pickled herring while the rest of the world eats smoked salmon," one voter explained.

Back in 2055, the Global Council predicted it would take three years to bring all the nations together into one Confederation with one world government and one currency. It has taken longer than expected, but spokesperson Maria Cravioto (from Section 2, formerly Mexico) says the Confederation should include all the world's nations by the year 2068. Meanwhile, Easter Island is expected to be the next country to come on board. Can it be long before the moon and planets join too?

Family Trapped in Computerized Home

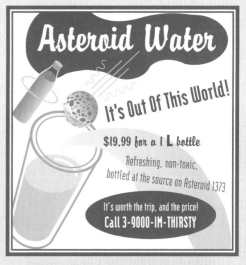

by EFREN LEBLANC

Another ICM Comp Home™ has gone haywire in Area 17 of Section 11 (formerly Winnipeg, Canada). Residents of the home—Larry Lex and his children, Dex and Lil—were trapped inside for three weeks. The ICM company is stumped. "There must be an electrical problem in this area," says head technician Terry Signoretti. "We're continuing to investigate."

The Lex family are now out, and safe. Mr. Lex says: "We'll never go back in there. At first, we couldn't make any calls or send e-mail. Then the security system wouldn't let us leave the house. We were completely cut off from the rest of the world! Finally, the computer went completely crazy and stopped supplying us with heat and food. Things were getting really desperate. I don't think I could ever go back to living in a Comp Home."

Longer School Year Approved

by MERRY MERIDIAN

Education Ministers from all school districts for Section 11 (formerly Canada) have announced a 324-day school year. IQ Minister Ali Hassan says that research done in other sections proves that students benefit from this extended school year. "Children achieve higher grades, finish school much earlier, and join the work force well prepared," he claims.

*(See **Surveys** on page **58**)*

(Surveys from page 57)

Surveys report that most parents are looking forward to this new, longer school year. So for millions of children, it's back to school with two weeks off for winter break and two weeks off for summer break this year.

Robots Get Straight A's From Teachers and Kids

by SKIP CURTIS

Clever study robots (models K5 and 3Rs) are taking the classroom by storm and both teachers and students are thrilled. These robots can complete homework faster than five kids put together. "Mine works great," says 11-year-old Colli Vaughan.

"I'd never get my schoolwork done without it!"

Teacher Rashid Morgan agrees, "I think these robots are wonderful. If my students can program them to get their work done in half the time, it's fine with me!"

A recent survey shows that most children would rather have a study robot than a personal jet.

S P O R T S

Robo Cup Debate Continues

by ALDO CLARKE

Human soccer players continue their legal battle with the Robot World Cup Organizers today. The human players have taken their fight to the Soccer Council (or Football Council) in Section 7 (formerly England). The human players are complaining that they're losing their jobs as a result of the popularity of Robot Soccer. "We can't find any work as professional soccer players," says Chris "Kicks" Chang, a former soccer goalie. "We can't compete physically with those robot players—they're just too strong, too tough." The trial continues next week.

The Great One's Granddaughter Back On Ice

by LAURA ZOKO

Colleen Gretzky, granddaughter of Dwayne Gretzky, "The Great One," has signed a four-month, eight-million-dollar deal to play forward centre for the Section 9 team (formerly Italy) next season in the Universal Hockey League.

Gretzky began her career in Area 21 of Section 4 (formerly California, United States) playing for the Colts. Since earthquakes and rising ocean levels have made that area unsafe, she and her family have moved to Area 14 of Section 11 (formerly Calgary, Canada), where her grandfather's career began. Colleen plans to fly her own jet from her zebra ranch to hockey games and practices.

 Click here for recent hockey stats.

Jaxson Warms Up

by LOLA ROLAND

Twentieth-century entertainer Michael Jaxson was thawed out Friday at his lab in Section 3 (formerly Japan). Jaxson's first words were, "Are my CDs still selling?"

His publicist said that Jaxson hopes to be back in the recording studio as soon as he's completely warmed up. Jaxson topped the international pop music charts in the Ancient Eighties. At the turn of the century, he chose to have his body frozen so he could stage the biggest comeback in rock-and-roll history!

 Click here for a complete list of song titles.

McDoogle's Serves All Nine Planets

by CLARY JONES

PLUTO PLATTER 3000.0
SOLAR SANDWICH ... 4505.0
FOUR-STAR-FRIES 2225.00
ANTI-MATTER
WITH SPECIAL SAUCE ..5001.0

The United Food Organization announced today that a McDoogle's restaurant will soon open on the planet Pluto. By the end of the year, Pluto's citizens will be able to enjoy McDoogle's mouth-watering one hundred percent vegetarian meals. Pluto is the last planet in the earth's solar system to get a McDoogle's restaurant.

 Click here for reservations.

Fly The Historic *Pathfinder*

by MICHAEL AURORA

Need something to do on a rainy day? Why not put on your goggles and take a tour of the Virtual Space Museum. This month the feature exhibit is the *Mars Pathfinder*, one of NASA's first exploration vehicles. This interactive display allows you to fly to Mars with the *Pathfinder* and explore its surface, just as they did in the old days. In 1997, the *Pathfinder* picked up a few Martian rocks that had scientists almost convinced there was life on Mars (we know better now!). This sample of ancient space technology will be of interest to the whole family.

FADS AND TRENDS

- Global kids are crazy about the hot new video game *Black Holes and Blunderbusters™*.

- No trendy athlete is caught performing without the latest sports footwear—Growdidas. These shoes can raise your height by half a metre with a sharp kick to the toe button.

- Fashions from the Nutty Nineties are now back in fashion. Desirable duds include oversized denims—once essential for all teen skateboarders.

Computers On Hand

COMPACT 5000 COMPUTER

by YASOO PORTER

The Greatwall Computer Company announced today that their new hand-held computer will be released tomorrow—one month ahead of schedule. The softball-sized computer works by voice recognition and is entirely without buttons or keys. It can perform over eighty functions when it hears the correct code. Since it responds to any voice—even your toddler's—you'd better keep this handy computer on a high shelf! Company president Xero Chang says this latest model could make her as successful as computer whiz and ex-Confederation leader Phil Gates.

CLASSIFIED AD

RESPONDING
to LIFE IN 2060

FOLLOW UP

How old will you be in 2060? What do you think your life will be like then?

Understanding the Article

Looking Ahead

- Life is certainly different in 2060! Which of the changes would you like to see happen? Which ones would you consider bad news?
- Fill in the details: Does Colleen Gretzky play on a woman's team or a mixed team? Will Michael Jaxson's comeback be a success? Will vegetarian fast food ever become popular?
- Think of the various sections in this newspaper. What other sections do newspapers often have?

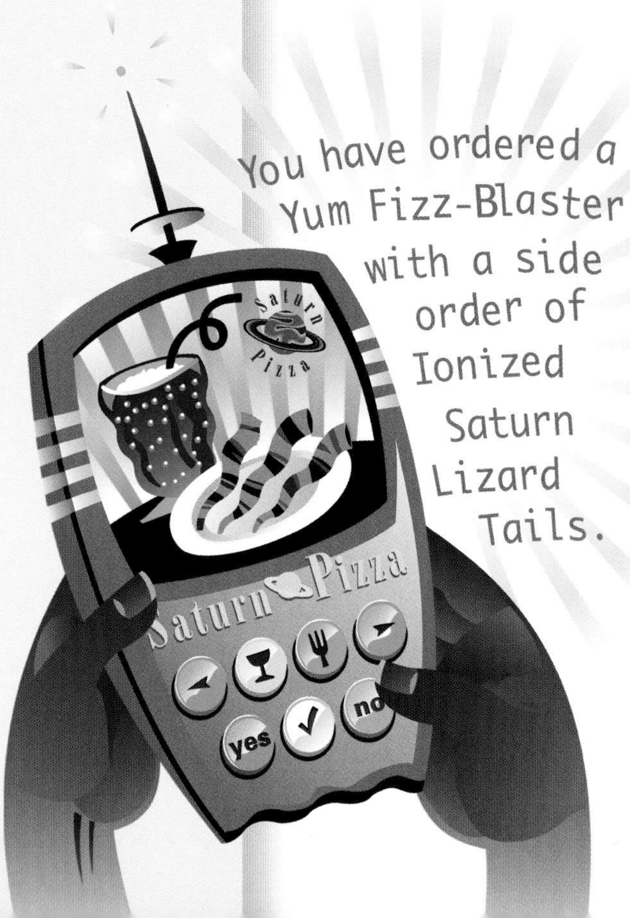

You have ordered a Yum Fizz-Blaster with a side order of Ionized Saturn Lizard Tails.
Saturn Pizza
Saturn Pizza
yes
no

YOUR TURN TO WRITE

Future Forms

In *Life in 2060,* you can see how articles and ads might look—and what they might say—in the future. What do you think other forms of writing will be like? For example, a menu for a restaurant, a love song, a Web site, a how-to article, or the label on a jar of peanut butter. Choose one of these, or another form, and create a future version of it. Share your writing with others.

IMAGINE!

You're a reporter in the year 2060 and the biggest news story of the century has just broken. What's happened? Write an article about this event.

Something To Think About

The article suggests that soccer-playing robots could replace human soccer players. Other jobs may also be lost as robots and computers begin to take over jobs that were traditionally done by humans. What do you think are the disadvantages of this? What are the advantages? How do you think the future of employment will be affected?

Media Link

Create a Class Newspaper

Develop a future newspaper. Choose one of the following jobs:

Editors: collect and edit the articles

Writers: research and write articles for Sports, Entertainment, Life and Leisure, and other sections

Reporters: research and write news stories

Designers: choose type styles, headline sizes, and artwork

Illustrators and Photographers: get images to support the articles

Step 1: As a group, decide on a name and date for the newspaper, and discuss what the future will be like.

Step 2: Reporters and writers submit ideas to the editors and then write the articles.

Step 3: Photographers and illustrators submit their work to the designers.

Step 4: Editors and designers work together to assemble the paper.

Step 5: Proofread each other's work before you publish your newspaper. Share your paper with others.

 TECH LINK

Post your newspaper on the school's Web site.

What are the best and worst things about cars today? How might cars of the future be different? Read and examine the labelled diagram of this Smart Car to discover how some experts think cars will change in the future.

Diagram by **Michael Herman**

Road to the FUTURE
The Smart Car

Hi! I'm a car of the 21st century and, wow, am I smart! I have miniature cameras and sensors. They tell my computer where other cars are, and if any obstacles are lying on the road ahead. With cars as smart as me on the road, accidents will be easy to avoid.

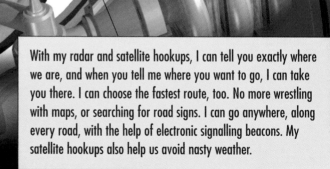

With my radar and satellite hookups, I can tell you exactly where we are, and when you tell me where you want to go, I can take you there. I can choose the fastest route, too. No more wrestling with maps, or searching for road signs. I can go anywhere, along every road, with the help of electronic signalling beacons. My satellite hookups also help us avoid nasty weather.

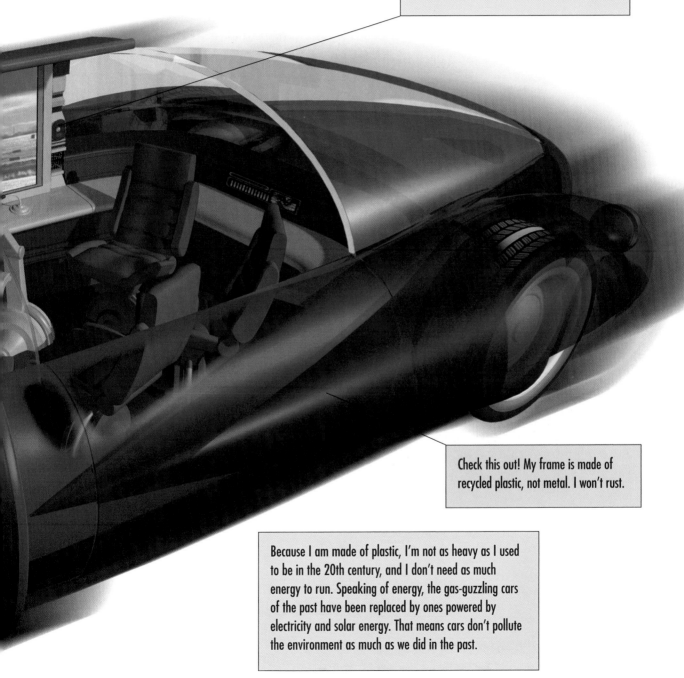

Notice I have no steering wheel? That's because future cars don't need steering wheels. We drive ourselves. You humans can just sit back and read a good book, or browse the Internet. But if you ever want to drive yourself, hey! just use the joystick. Driving in the future is as easy as playing a video game!

You may have noticed that my computer has a speaker and a microphone; that's because I'm smart enough to talk or listen to you, in any one of forty languages. So if you're hot, cold, or bored of driving on the highway, just let me know. I'll turn on the air conditioning, the heat, or the entertainment system.

Check this out! My frame is made of recycled plastic, not metal. I won't rust.

Because I am made of plastic, I'm not as heavy as I used to be in the 20th century, and I don't need as much energy to run. Speaking of energy, the gas-guzzling cars of the past have been replaced by ones powered by electricity and solar energy. That means cars don't pollute the environment as much as we did in the past.

FOLLOW UP

What information about cars in the future surprised you? How else do you think cars will change? Do you think these changes will be good or bad? Explain your answer.

YOUR TURN TO WRITE

A Labelled Diagram

With your classmates, discuss the advantages and disadvantages of the cars of the present, and of the Smart Car. Now imagine your ideal car (or bike, or train, or plane) of the future.

Next, draw a rough diagram and add point-form labels to show the vehicle's special features. (If you're not a very good artist, you might want to work with a partner who is, or use a computer art program to help you.) Show your first draft to another classmate and ask for feedback. Now draw a final draft, using colour, and writing more detailed labels. Display your diagram on a bulletin board with other vehicles of the future.

Understanding the Diagram

Drive On!

- What features of the Smart Car do you like? Of these, which is the most amazing?

- Is there anything you don't like about this car? Explain.

- In what ways is the Smart Car better for the environment?

- Do you think it will ever be possible to build a car like this one? Give reasons to support your opinion.

Summarize the Main Idea

In the diagram, each paragraph states one main idea about the Smart Car. For each paragraph, write a one-word heading in your notebook.

It's the year 2020 and you're "driving" a Smart Car. The computer suddenly breaks down. What happens? Write a complaint report to the car company.

Design a Poster:
Alternative Transportation

Many people think the future would be a better place to live if there were fewer cars on the road—since cars burn gas, which produces pollution. They want to see more bicycles and public transportation (streetcars, buses, trains, subways). What would you do to persuade people to give up cars and try an alternative form of transportation? Design a poster that makes the switch from cars to this form look attractive.

Car Ads

Watch for car ads on TV, in newspapers, or in magazines. Choose an example that appeals to you. Then develop an ad for a car of the future. Remember that the purpose of any ad is to sell the product, but it should also give information about the car's special features.

If you choose a TV ad, work with several classmates to develop a script. Then present your ad to the whole class.

If you're developing a print ad, use art and text (including a slogan—a catchy phrase) to "sell" your future car. Share your print ad with others.

BEFORE READING

Do you think life in the future will be better or worse than life today? Read on to find out what a famous science fiction writer thinks home, school, and the world could be like in the future.

Chris AND Sandy

Story by
Monica Hughes

Illustrations by
Odile Ouellet

"What are you studying in school today?" Father asked politely. He asked this same question every morning before returning to his study to work on the long mathematical calculations that would one day set the world right.

"Act Two of *Hamlet.* Plane Geometry. The causes of the First World War. Father, we're out of jam."

"Jam?" Father looked vaguely surprised, as if jam were a substance he had never heard of before. "Jam. I suppose we could have run out. We should go through the storeroom and bring our list up to date some time." He wandered off, his thumb marking the place in the book he had been reading during breakfast.

Too bad you couldn't hold a normal conversation with Father. It wasn't his fault. He was just too far inside his own head. Chris sighed. He tidied the kitchen and made a note to himself to check through the stores one day soon. Thank goodness for Sandy. Without Sandy he'd go crazy for sure.

He found his books, sat down at the table, and tapped EM Four's code into the computer. "Hello, EM Four. Chris ready for work. Is Sandy there yet?" Sandy was always late.

"Good morning, Chris. Please open your book at page fourteen. Act Two, Scene One: a room in Polonius's house...Here is Sandy."

On the TV screen appeared a picture of a freckled boy, about twelve or thirteen years old, with a wide grin.

"Hi, Chris, what's cooking?"

"Hi, Sandy. Not much. Did you get all your homework done last night?"

The voice of the computer cut in. "Shall we begin, boys? Chris, explain the meaning of the scene between Ophelia and her father. How does it advance the plot?"

"Well, I guess Ophelia's scared of Hamlet because he's—" On the TV screen Sandy crossed his eyes, wiggled his ears, and put out his tongue. Chris snorted with laughter and wondered if EM Four knew what games Sandy got up to when they were supposed to be working.

"I don't think Hamlet's mad. I think it's just a put-on," Sandy interrupted.

"Give me your reasons, Chris," EM Four said calmly.

"Oh, I don't know. It just strikes me that way, that's all."

The lesson finished, and Chris reached over to the cupboard and got a glass of synthetic milk and a protein cracker. Sandy said he'd go and get a snack too. Chris stared at the blank screen while he drank his milk and wished it would show the inside of Sandy's house. There was only a blank wall behind Sandy's cheery face, and Chris had never seen his friend's home.

When he got back, Chris asked him, "Exactly where do you live?"

"On top of the hill. Not far."

"It'd be such fun if we could get together."

"We're together now. There's school and chess games and—"

"It's not the same thing. You know, Sandy, sometimes I get absolutely squirrelly, stuck in the house all day with just Father."

"You have me for company too," EM Four put in. "No more talking now, boys. Time for Geometry. Chris, will you enumerate the properties of triangles?"

After math there was History, and then the TV closed down. Chris picked a package marked "SKL #1" for his lunch and sat down at the table to eat it, staring at the empty screen. He

wished Sandy would stay and have lunch with him, but always, as soon as lessons were over, he vanished and only reappeared when Chris coded "Games Time" into the computer. A long, empty afternoon stretched in front of him. He sighed and pushed away the rest of his lunch.

"I wish I could go over to his house. Give him one heck of a surprise if I turned up there." He found himself walking out of the room and staring at the big front door.

For years there had been a red light over it, but about five months ago the light had turned green. When Chris had told Father, he had said vaguely, "It makes no difference. We have all we need here."

Maybe it was true for him, but it sure wasn't for Chris— thirteen years old, skinny, and growing fast, needing leg room.

Almost without meaning to, he began to turn the great wheel in the centre of the door. The first half-turn was almost more than he could manage, but then it became easier. He spun it round and round, and at last, with a faint creak, the door swung inward.

He stepped through, his heart beating hard, into a masonry shaft with metal hoops set into the wall. They led, like a staircase, up into the gloom, where he could faintly see another door, really more of a lid, sealing the top of the shaft.

Chris hesitated. Should he tell Father what he planned to do? But the study door was firmly shut. Even as a little boy, when Mother was still alive, the one rule had been: Father must never be disturbed.

"But why? I need him to play with us, Mom."

"He's working on special problems, and when he's got the answers, the world will be a safer place to live in. He's a genius, Chris, and he mustn't be disturbed."

He could almost hear Mother's voice. He set his foot to the first hoop and reached up for a handhold. Rust came off bright orange, and the hoops trembled beneath his weight, but they held. He climbed up into the shadows that came down over his shoulders like a dusty shawl.

At the top he spun the wheel in the lid and set his shoulder to it. The hoop on which he was standing bent beneath the pressure, and he grabbed at the wheel, sweating and trembling. It was a very long way down. Then he set his feet apart, one on each of the two hoops, to spread the weight of his body, and tried again, heaving with all his strength against the metal lid.

It creaked, moved, lifted, and he straightened his back and pushed with both hands. It fell back with a clang, a clatter of stones, and a cloud of bitter stone dust. Slowly Chris climbed out into sunlight.

It shone in bright bars through a broken wall with dust dancing in it. The light was so strong, his eyes ran and he sneezed. He crawled cautiously between two jagged segments of wall like ruined teeth and looked around.

Below him was a desolate expanse of grey, the grey of powdered concrete and brick, grey and thick as a carpet, curved by the wind into frozen waves that seemed to beat silently against the hill on which he stood.

"Up on the hill." "Not far." "The house on the corner with the red roof and the black trim." "With the white picket fence." Chris remembered the small descriptions Sandy had let slip over the years of their friendship. Even, long ago, "A tree in the backyard with a super swing."

There were no trees up here. No swings. No houses. No streets.

The wind shivered and lifted the dust around his bare ankles. The sky was cloudless, a bowl of harsh blue from the centre of which the sun burned down.

Chris climbed down the shaft, carefully closing the lid behind him. There would be no visitors. He brushed the dust off his legs before entering the house and shutting the big front door. The house hummed quietly. The lights shone, comfortably dim.

He hesitated at the door of the study. But what was the use? He went into the other room and slumped at the table. After a time he punched EM Four's code into the computer.

"Hello, Chris. What can I do for you?"

"You lied to me."

"I? In what way?"

"I've been outside. Sandy's not real. He never could have been there, could he? My only friend, and he's not real." He put his head down on his arms.

"He is real, Chris, truly."

"Oh, sure. Where does he live then? Come on, EM Four, I'm not stupid."

"Sandy is here in this shelter."

"What?" Chris jumped to his feet. "Where? How could he be? Come on, show me where he is."

"He is difficult to reach sometimes. When you are angry—"

"I'm not angry. I am *not* angry." Chris pounded his fist on the table.

"It was not good for you to grow up alone. After your mother's death you needed a companion to keep you healthy and happy, to give meaning to your life."

"Then you *did* invent him. He *is* a lie."

"No. All I did was bring him out."

Chris slumped at the table. "Are you trying to be difficult? No, don't answer that, I can't stand it. EM Four, how many people are still living."

"You and your father are the only life forms I have been able to detect. But my range is quite limited. There is no reason to doubt—"

"Then you lied. Sandy isn't real." Tears leaked through his closed lids, and he put his head down again.

"Sandy *is* real. Listen to me, Chris. Sandy is *you*. The part of yourself that liked to have fun, that didn't want to study—the adventurous part. The part that remembered a swing and a picket fence. Sandy is *inside you*."

Chris stared through his tears at the blank screen, remembering the freckled boy who could wiggle his ears. He felt as if someone he loved had died.

That night he lay in his narrow bunk above the table and listened to the steady whisper of the air conditioner. When the clock told him it was morning, he got up and made breakfast for Father and himself, as he had done every other day.

"What are you studying today?" Father asked, his eyes still on the papers he had brought from his study. Chris thought of telling him about Sandy, but it seemed kind of useless.

"How close are you?"

"Eh?"

"To a solution, Father."

"Oh, my goodness, that's hard to say. I see a glimmer, you know, at the end of the tunnel. A glimmer."

"What'll you do with the solution when you've found it?"

"Do? Why...I don't know... That is for others to decide—physicists, astronomers. My work is to advance the frontier of knowledge. What other people do with it is up to them." He wandered back to his study. The door shut.

Chris cleared away the breakfast dishes and sat down at the computer terminal. He sighed and then punched in EM Four's code. "Ready for work," he said and reached for his *Hamlet*.

As he read, he found himself looking at the empty TV screen. When he stared at the printed page, dust motes danced in the golden sun at the top of the shaft. He shut the book.

"EM Four, is Sandy there?"

At once Sandy's face filled the screen—the wide grin, the twinkle in the eyes. "Hi, fella, I thought you'd given up on me."

"Fat chance. Listen, Sandy, I'm sick of *Hamlet* and Geometry and the causes of the First World War. What about a study on how to find other people and learn to start living again?"

"I thought you'd never ask, Chris. EM Four, are you listening? Help! We've got a lot to learn."

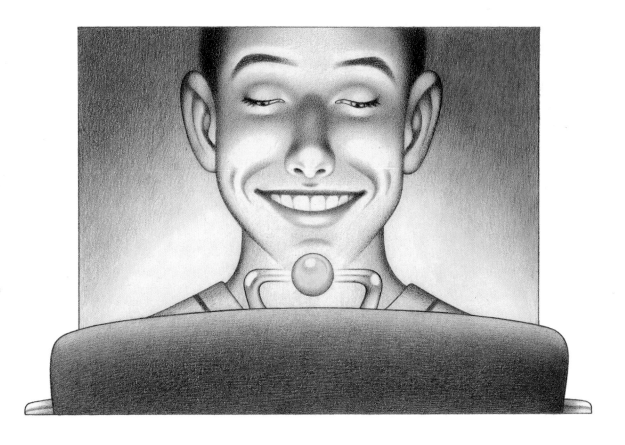

FOLLOW UP

With a partner, discuss how Chris's life is different from your own. How is it the same? How would you describe the future world that Monica Hughes creates in her story?

Author Study

Monica Hughes has written many novels for young adults, such as *Space Trap*, *The Golden Aquarians*, *The Refuge*, and *The Isis Pedlar*. If you like science fiction, or would like to give science fiction a try, read one of these novels.

With a small group of classmates, hold a book talk. Discuss the author's vision of the future, the exciting adventure her characters have, and the story's message.

Understanding the Story

Dark Visions

- Why does Chris feel that he can't hold a normal conversation with his father? What is his father busy doing?

- What is school like for Chris and Sandy? Do their lessons seem to be useful to them?

- Why do you think the red light over the door has turned green?

- How do you think Chris feels when he sees the world outside his door?

- How does EM Four explain who Sandy is? What other important fact does he tell Chris about the world outside?

- What does Chris decide to do at the end of the story? Do you think this is a happy ending? Why or why not?

A Science Fiction Story

What events do you think led up to Chris and his father living the way they do? Write a science fiction story telling your version of these events. Then, if you like, continue the story into Chris's future.

WRITER'S CRAFT

Science Fiction

Many science fiction stories are set in the future, and include scientific or technological elements such as aliens, spaceships, robots, or sophisticated computers. With a small group, discuss how *Chris and Sandy* is both futuristic and based on modern technology. Describe the world that Monica develops in *Chris and Sandy*.

Science fiction stories can also get readers thinking about the consequences of events that are happening in the present. How is this statement true of this story? What does Monica want to warn her readers about?

Illustrate the Future

What do you think the place where you live will be like in the future? Ask family members to contribute their ideas, and then discuss these ideas with your classmates.

With your classmates, plan a multimedia collage that shows what life in the future will be like. Use photos, maps, your own artwork, and words and images cut from magazines and newspapers. Display your collage on a bulletin board. Share your collage and this story with family members and other classes.

Believe it or not, one of the hardest things to teach a robot is how to walk. Skim the title and subheadings in the following article and make a prediction: What creature from the animal world could help robot scientists solve this problem?

Magazine Article by STEVE MILLER

Adapted by CHRIS MCCLYMONT

Robot Critters

Walking Like Bugs

Next time you get the chance, watch a slow-moving insect (like a daddy-longlegs) walk over rough ground. You'll notice that as each leg moves, it feels around for firm footing, moving up or down or sideways to find the best spot. It also reacts to the position of the legs beside it. This is a very complex series of movements. Robot scientists would be thrilled if robots could walk as well as bugs can.

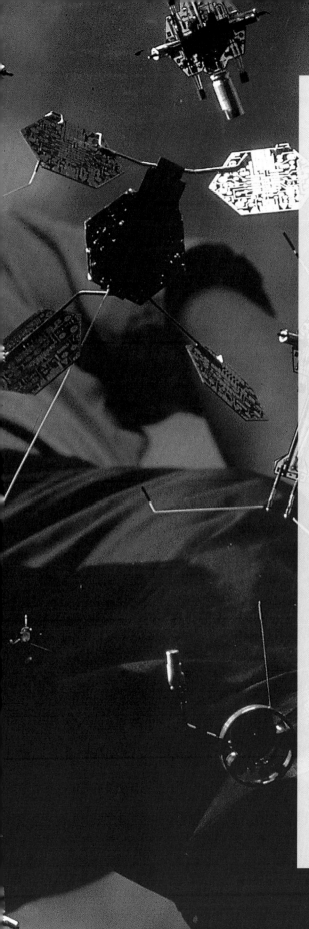

When you think of walking robots, you may imagine C-3PO in the movie *Star Wars*, walking on two legs like a person. But most robots of today can't walk on two legs. They have to calculate how to keep their balance all the time—an incredible problem. To get some idea of what robots face, try walking very slowly, and pay attention to how many balance adjustments you need to make to keep from falling.

Robots that can walk usually have six or eight legs, like an insect or a spider. Multi-legs offer a much more stable design. To help robot critters make balance calculations, a separate microprocessor (or computer chip) controls each leg. All the microprocessors are linked to each other so that the motion of one leg is affected—but not controlled—by the legs next to it. This is just the way a daddy-longlegs walks!

Robot Critters at Work

Why do we need walking robots? Most robots stay in one spot to do their jobs. Robots in car factories use their "arms" to place car parts in the right position or weld parts together. But many jobs require a mobile robot to do things that are too dangerous—or even impossible—for humans to do.

For example, Robug III inspects and maintains the inside of a nuclear reactor, a very dangerous job for people. Robug III is a buglike robot that was designed in England. It's big for a bug, weighing about 100 kg. But Robug can make its way over rough surfaces, and even climb walls, just like a real bug.

Scientists in New Mexico are working on tiny robots called MARVs (Miniature Autonomous Robotic Vehicles). Their job will be to search for land mines and detonate them. Each MARV would be blown up with the land mine it detonates, but the robot critter can be built for only a few dollars, and many lives could be saved.

Real bugs can walk, but they don't usually go where you ask them to go. Enter the bionic cockroach. An engineer in Tokyo has built a very special electronic backpack that connects directly to the cockroach's nervous system—making it a remote-control bug! In the future, bionic cockroaches could inspect the insides of pipes or look for people trapped in collapsed buildings.

By 2010, scientists expect that tiny robots called **microbots** will perform surgery. Patients will swallow pills with microbots inside. The robot critters, equipped with mini-cameras, will head to the intestines, lungs, or other organs to dissolve tumours. Really tiny microbots (the size of a grain of rice) will swim inside arteries and clear away the harmful deposits that cause heart disease. But before microbots can really work, they need a certain amount of intelligence. Scientists think the intelligence level of ants would do the trick!

Keep Studying Bugs

Although robot scientists have learned a lot from studying insects, they can't yet duplicate them. The design of the simplest insect is still much more complicated than the most advanced robot. In the future, look to the insect world for more lessons on robotics!

> " When it comes to walking, the lowly cockroach outperforms the most sophisticated robot at every turn! "
>
> *Randall Beer, robot scientist*

Robot Time Line

1921 The word **robot** is used for the first time in a play called R. U. R. *(Rossum's Universal Robots)* by Karel Capek of the Czech Republic.

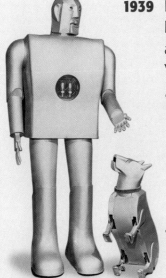

1939 Electro, a giant robot, and his robot dog, Spark, (left) are exhibited at the New York World's Fair.

1954 The first industrial robot, built by George Duvol, is a huge mechanical version of a human arm.

1969 SHAKEY, a wobbly robot that moves on wheels, is built in California. It has sensors on its bumpers, a swivelling head, a TV-camera eye, and a radio link to a computer. SHAKEY can plan a route and move obstacles out of its way to reach its destination.

1976 *Viking 1* lands on Mars. Its robotic arm collects soil samples to bring back to scientists.

1977 The movie *Star Wars* introduces the popular robot characters R-2D2 and C-3P0 to the world.

1981 The robot-like Canadarm takes its first flight on a space shuttle. With its flexible joints, the arm can lift heavy loads into and out of the cargo bay. Its computer-operated "brain" allows it to be operated automatically or by an astronaut working outside the shuttle.

1983 Six-legged Odex-1 becomes the first walking robot to be sold in stores.

1986 The robotic vehicle Jason, Jr. (above) explores the wreckage of the *Titanic* at the bottom of the Atlantic Ocean.

1997 The robotic *Pathfinder* (below) explores Mars, sending messages back to Earth.

Which of the robot critters seemed to you to be the most surprising? the most fun? the most useful? What would you still like to know about robots?

Understanding the Article

Do the Bug Walk

- Why are six- or eight-legged robots more effective walkers than two-legged ones?

- Think of at least one more useful job that each of these robot critters could do: Robug III, MARV, the bionic cockroach, microbots.

- Robot scientists are studying many kinds of bugs. What might they learn from ants? bees? butterflies? mosquitoes? or other interesting insects?

- In your opinion, which three dates on the Robot Time Line are the most important? Explain your answer.

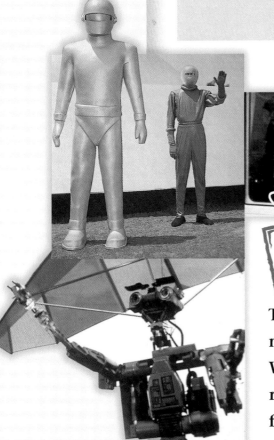

Robots pictured here are from the movies *The Day the Earth Stood Still* (top left); *The Empire Strikes Back* (top right); and *Short Circuit* (bottom).

Media Link Movie Robots

Think of some robots you've seen on TV shows, or in movies. What were they like? How did they move? What could they do? What couldn't they do? Are robots usually the heroes or villains? Do they ever feel emotions? Write a short proposal for an exciting children's movie starring good and bad robots.

Find Out More About...

With a partner, research one of the robots listed in the Robot Time Line using library or Internet resources. Find out as much about this robot as you can, and share your information with others. Organize your notes under these headings:

- Date and Place of Manufacture
- Designer/Inventor
- Materials
- Purpose/Skills
- Special Features
- Strengths and Weaknesses

A Time Line

Develop a time line for another modern invention, such as computers or TV. Add to your time line your ideas about what the future will hold for this product. Also include illustrations or photos. Share your time line with others.

 TECH LINK
Multimedia software can help you create an interactive presentation.

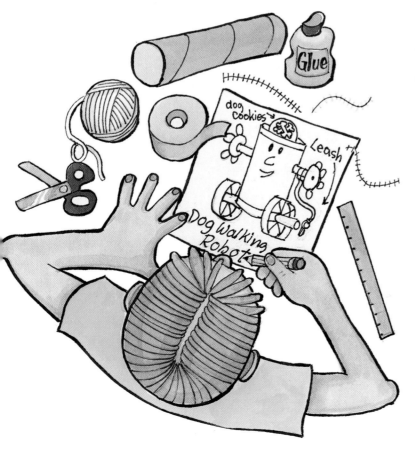

Design a Robot

What job would you like a robot to do for you? Walk the dog? Cut the lawn? Tidy your room? Design a robot that will do this job. Begin with a sketch, with labels to explain special features. Then use art and scrap materials (pipe cleaners, tape, string, cardboard tubes, and so on) to build your robot—your imagination is the only limit. Share your robot with your family and classmates, explaining what it can do.

ON TO FUTURE

BEFORE READING

When astronaut and scientist Dr. Roberta Bondar travelled into space on the *Discovery* space shuttle, she had to deal with cramped quarters, floating tools, nausea, and space food! Here's the inside scoop on eating in microgravity.

SPACED-OUT
Food

Article by
BARBARA BONDAR,
with
DR. ROBERTA BONDAR

Dr. Roberta Bondar became Canada's first female astronaut when she was launched into space on board the *Discovery* space shuttle on January 22, 1992. This mission was the first flight of the International Microgravity Laboratory (IML-1). Roberta's job was to carry out fifty-five experiments, including testing the effects of low gravity on taste and blood pressure.

"It's important to advance the use of space as a new environment for science, to answer questions we can't answer on Earth."

Dr. Roberta Bondar

Roberta (left) begins an experiment in the IML-1.

As soon as *Discovery* is in orbit around the Earth, the crew feel the first effects of being in microgravity. They seem to float, and so do any loose objects in the shuttle. So everything the astronauts do is a challenge, especially eating! Come along and experience the difficulties—and the fun—with Roberta and the rest of the crew.

- The mid-deck of *Discovery* is about 4 m by 4.5 m. Within this small area are the sleeping cabinets and washroom—and the crew's galley. The galley is where all the food is stored and heated. Five to eight months before the launch of shuttle IML-1, food scientists arranged food-tasting sessions. Each member of the seven-member crew chose every item for every one of their meals. The scientists evaluated the food to be sure the astronauts would be getting the proper caloric intake on the mission.

  The mid-deck doesn't look much like a kitchen. There is no freezer or cooking oven for the crew's food. It would take up too much of the crew's living space. There is a small heating unit for warming food, though, and the galley dispenses hot or cold water.

- The crew doesn't chow down on baked potatoes or steaks in the orbiter's galley. Although small pieces of potato and beef can be freeze-dried and included in several of the crew's dishes, scientists haven't yet figured out how to freeze-dry large food items.

Dr. Roberta Bondar
Payload Specialist*

- Born December 4th, 1945, Sault Ste Marie, Ontario
- Canadian Space Agency Astronaut
- First shuttle flight
- Three degrees in science (B.S., M.S., Ph.D.)
- Degree in medicine (M.D.)
- Pilot, neurologist, space flight surgeon

*Payload Specialists are astronauts who are responsible for science experiments. Mission Specialists are astronauts who operate and maintain the shuttle and Spacelab systems.

Lunchtime! Mission specialist Norman Thagard digs into a food tray to find what he wants to eat. For a hot meal, he can heat his food in the open heating unit up on his right.

Ulf Merbold, one of the crew, examines a perfect sphere of floating grapefruit juice he has squeezed from his juice bag. (On Earth, the drops would be teardrop-shaped because gravity is pulling down on the liquid in the drop.) To drink the juice, Ulf needs to insert a straw into the drop, then suck it up—a tricky manoeuvre.

How do astronauts make a freeze-dried meal edible? They rehydrate* it. First they stick a needle into a freeze-dried food pack and inject a pre-selected amount of hot or cold water. Then they knead or shake the food until it is thoroughly moistened. Next, the astronauts snip around the plastic with surgical scissors to make an opening big enough for a spoon—and then it's time to dig in.

- "The sauce is loose!" The alert comes from Roberta Bondar, who has let the shrimp cocktail sauce lose contact with her spoon.

  Food particles of any kind can be a problem in microgravity. They don't drop to the ground. Until they are recaptured, they hang in the air and could be dangerous if they find their way into someone's eye, nose, or ear. They can also infect and ruin experiments and interrupt electrical circuits. To be safe, most of the solid food sent into space is naturally moist. The moister the food, the fewer the crumbs. (Luckily, food escapes didn't happen very often on this flight.)

- There are no baked beans or large amounts of broccoli or mushrooms on the crew's menu. Why not? They might cause the crew to experience gas pains. Gas pains are more painful in space and could be potentially dangerous as scientists still aren't sure how gases behave in microgravity.

---

*Astronauts' food is dehydrated—the water is taken out—so that it doesn't go bad. It is then **rehydrated**—the water is put back in—when it's time to eat it.

Dr. Roberta Bondar rounds up the necessary ingredients for a tortilla snack.

- What are the crew's favourite meals? Shrimp cocktail with sauce, tortillas with peanut butter or cheese spreads, and chicken dishes. Items from the fresh food locker are pretty popular, too. The day before lift-off, it was packed with candies, sweets and snacks, relish, cookies, chewing gum, and apples.

- Space is a great place to play with your food. In microgravity, the astronauts can twirl carrot sticks, swallow a floating sphere of sauce, and send a half-peeled banana spinning across the mid-deck with its peel sticking out like propeller blades.

Space Technology in Our Lives

Experiments conducted in space and the experience of living on space shuttle flights have had many benefits for life on Earth. Here is a small part of an ever-growing list of items originally created for space:

- rehydratable foods, such as ice cream
- special foam for ski boots, football pads, and helmets
- thermal gloves, boots, and blankets
- smoke detectors
- cushioning used in athletic shoes
- cordless drills and other tools
- scratch-resistant coatings for plastic lenses
- stick controls for physically challenged drivers
- low-intensity X ray imagers used in hospital emergency rooms.

List three facts about space food that you learned from this article.

Career Tip

ASTRONAUT

Where will astronauts be going in the future—Mars, Jupiter, Saturn, or other galaxies? Would you like to be an astronaut? You have to enjoy living in small spaces, eating space food, and be able to ride wild roller coasters without getting sick! If you want to become an astronaut, you should also

- **take math and science courses in school**
- **study a second language**
- **participate in science fairs**
- **visit a space museum**
- **develop good exercise habits**

Serving All Planets

As a whole class, host a Space Feast. Discuss the foods that were served on the shuttle, and how they were prepared. Gather the ingredients for some of these foods (some freeze-dried foods are available at camping stores) and prepare them to serve to your guests (other classes or family members). Design and print a menu for your Space Feast. Explain to your guests the reasons behind some of these space foods, and why the astronauts need a balanced, healthy diet.

Understanding the Article

High-Flying Menus

- Who is Dr. Roberta Bondar? Why is she a Canadian hero?

- What space foods listed in the article would you enjoy eating? Which would you definitely not enjoy?

- What important factors do scientists consider when planning the menu for each astronaut?

- Would a space flight be a good opportunity for a food fight? Why, or why not?

- Why is it important to dehydrate and then rehydrate the food?

Space Travel Research

The Canadarm

The *Sojourner* on Mars.

Work with three or four classmates to find out about one famous flight into space; for example, the very first space flight, or the first flight to land on the moon. Use library and Internet resources—check out the Canadian Space Agency's and NASA's Web sites! Present your research in a short report illustrated with photos and diagrams. Display your report with reports from other groups to present "A History of Space Travel."

Space Inventions

Some of the things we take for granted were invented for space flight (see page 87). Think of a new and useful invention that would help out space travellers. Draw and label a diagram of your invention. Share your invention with the whole class, explaining why it would be useful.

IMAGINE!
You be the scientist: What is your idea for a microgravity experiment that could be done on the next space shuttle flight?

Unique?

Poem by **Adrian Rumble**

How strange
to think
that somewhere
out in deepest space,
millions of years away,
there is
someone
who is just
like me.

Yet stranger still
to think
that nowhere
in all those
vast dark worlds
is there
anyone
who could be
like me.

RESPONDING

to UNIQUE?

Personal Response — Do you think there are other living creatures somewhere in the universe? If so, would they look like humans, or completely different? Do you think we will ever see them? Discuss your ideas with a partner.

How does poet Adrian Rumble feel about the possibility of life in outer space? Why does the poet choose the title *Unique?* Look up **unique** in a dictionary if you're not sure what it means.

Illustrating the Poem

What did you think of when you read the words "vast dark worlds"? Draw an illustration that captures how you felt when you read this poem. Share your illustration with your classmates, and discuss how you, and they, felt. Create a "Unique Art" display on a hall bulletin board.

Media Link — **Aliens!**

There are many TV shows and movies that feature aliens—invented creatures from other planets. Discuss these shows with two or three classmates. Choose one that you've seen recently, and discuss what makes the show believable or not. How are these aliens like us? How are they different? What makes the show work (or not work)? Together, develop a review for this show. Share your review with other classmates.

MORE GOOD READING

✤ **On the Shuttle: Eight Days in Space by Barbara Bondar and Dr. Roberta Bondar**

This book takes readers on a trip into space. Find out how the astronauts prepare for their flight, and what they do once they're up there. (a non-fiction book)

Spaceways edited by John Foster

An amusing collection of science fiction poems that explore the mysteries of space. (a poetry anthology)

The Great Robot Book by Wanda and Texe Marrs

In the future, many people believe robots will perform many tasks we dislike—like doing dishes and taking out the garbage. In this book, the authors explore some of the jobs robots will be able to do for us. (a non-fiction book)

Marvels
Then
and
Now

If You Want to See

POEM BY *Samantha Abeel*

If you want to see the past,
look around you
for everything you do is
living out the legacy of those
who came before you...

If you want to see the present,
look around you
for it is what you are building
for those who will come
after you...

If you want to see the future,
look inside you
for it is where all the building
begins.

Have you ever wondered what the Seven Wonders of the World are? Here's your chance to find out about the seven ancient wonders, and seven wonders you can still visit.

Article by
ROBERT CUTTING

Illustrations by
PAUL McCUSKER

Wonders of the World

I
Seven Wonders of the Ancient World

Over 2000 years ago, the Greeks and Romans made a list of the most spectacular buildings around the eastern shores of the Mediterranean Sea.

These marvels later became famous as the Seven Wonders of the World.

1. The Pyramids of Egypt

Built nearly 5000 years ago, the pyramids are the oldest of the seven ancient wonders of the world, and the only "wonder" still standing to the present day. The pyramids were built as tombs for the pharaohs (rulers) of Ancient Egypt. The Great Pyramid at Giza took thousands of workers about thirty years to build. It is 137 m high, and built of about two million blocks of stone, each weighing over 2 tonnes.

2. The Pharos of Alexandria

The first large lighthouse ever built, the white marble Pharos survived 1000 years and several earthquakes. At the top, a fire was kept burning day and night. An enormous mirror reflected the light so it could be seen 50 km out to sea. To many people, the Pharos symbolized the glory of Alexander the Great, who founded many cities— all named Alexandria after him. The greatest of all was in Egypt, where the Pharos was built.

3. The Hanging Gardens of Babylon

Stories about the hanging gardens called them an earthly paradise rising out of the desert. They were built 2000 years ago by King Nebuchadnezzar for his wife, who missed the hilly green landscape of her Persian homeland. A Roman writer described the gardens as a series of terraces, each containing enough soil for exotic flowers, palms, and cypress trees to grow. Today nothing is left of Babylon or the gardens, apart from a few ruins.

4. The Temple of Artemis

This temple in the Greek city of Ephesus was built in 550 B.C., then rebuilt 200 years later after a devastating fire. One of the largest temples of its time—52 m wide and 112 m long—it contained splendid sculptures of the goddess Artemis and other gods and heroes. Pictures on ancient coins tell us that it had two rows of 20-m columns. Over time, the temple's ruins disappeared, but its exact location was rediscovered in 1869.

5. The Mausoleum at Halicarnassus

King Mausolus ruled over part of modern-day Turkey in the 4th century B.C. Toward the end of his life, he decided to build himself a magnificent tomb in his new capital city of Halicarnassus. On the very top was a statue of the king in his chariot. Today, any grand tomb is called a **mausoleum** after Mausolus.

6. The Colossus of Rhodes

Around 300 B.C., the people of the Greek island of Rhodes built a statue of Helios, the sun god, at the entrance to their city harbour. Called the Colossus because of its "colossal" size, it rose 37 m high, but nobody knows exactly what it looked like. Archaeologists believe the statue had an iron framework covered with thin sheets of bronze, much like the modern Statue of Liberty. After sixty-five years, an earthquake sent the Colossus tumbling into the sea.

7. The Statue of Zeus

According to Greek mythology, Zeus was king of the gods. In 433 B.C., the Greek sculptor, Phidias, completed a magnificent statue of him. It was placed in a temple built especially for it in Olympia. About 12 m tall, the statue was carved out of ivory. Zeus's hair and beard were made of gold, and his eyes were precious gemstones. About 700 years later, the statue was probably taken to Constantinople (Istanbul), where it was destroyed by fire.

II
Seven Marvels You Can Visit Today

All over the world, there are ancient marvels that the Greeks and Romans never knew about. Here are just a few—and some modern marvels, too. All of these wonders still exist, and tourists flock to see them.

1. Easter Island, South Pacific

If you sail 3747 km west from South America into the South Pacific Ocean, you will eventually arrive at Easter Island. The island is so remote that it was not discovered by the outside world until Easter Sunday, 1722. Those first European explorers were greeted with a true marvel: almost 800 colossal statues, from 2 to 10 m in height, weighing up to 83 tonnes. Most of them face into the island, turning their backs to the ocean. They were carved between 500 and 1000 years ago. As archaeologists learn more, the mystery of why the statues were made will one day be revealed.

2. Great Zimbabwe*, Africa

This extraordinary collection of stone buildings, walls, and towers was once a capital city in the country we now call Zimbabwe. Built by the Shona people around A.D. 1350, it was the residence of the most powerful ruler in south-eastern Africa. Within the city, the high walls of the Great Enclosure were built from one million granite stones. Inside lived five or six families related to the king. One striking feature in the enclosure is a stone tower, 10 m high—possibly a symbol of the king's power. Great Zimbabwe had a population of more than 10 000 people. The city was mysteriously abandoned in A.D. 1450.

*Zimbabwe** means "stone house" or "chief's house" in the Shona language.

3. The Tomb of the Emperor Ch'in, China

In 1974, workers digging near the city of Xian were amazed to discover thousands of life-size statues. They turned out to be a vast, underground army of terra cotta soldiers guarding the tomb of the Emperor Ch'in Shi Huang-ti (259-209 B.C.). More than 700 000 labourers worked for thirty-six years building the huge tomb. Almost 8000 statues have been found in three burial pits. Each footman, bowman, spearman, and officer has a unique face. On average, the figures are 1.8 m tall, with hollow bodies and solid limbs. Today, hundreds of thousands of visitors view the statues every year.

4. Machu Picchu, Peru

High in the Andes Mountains lies the deserted fortress city of Machu Picchu. Once the home of 1000 people, it was built by the Incas during the 15th century A.D. At that time, the Inca emperor ruled over eight million people. Sheer cliffs on three sides helped to defend the city, while a deep, dry moat and high stone walls protected the fourth side. Within the city, more than 3000 steps linked its houses, temples, and palaces. The stone building blocks were made so accurately that you can hardly see the cracks in between them.

5. Taj Mahal, India

The Taj Mahal is one of the world's most beautiful and romantic tombs. The story goes that Shah Jahan, a 17th-century emperor, was heartbroken when his wife, Mumtaz-i-Mahal, died in childbirth. He vowed to build a magnificent tomb in her memory. It took 20 000 workers twenty-two years to build the white marble structure with its onion-shaped dome, slender towers, and gem-encrusted interior. Today, visitors still walk toward the fairy-tale monument through a beautiful walled garden. A long pool reflects the building. The colour of the marble changes according to the weather and time of day.

6. Sydney Opera House, Australia

Visitors to Sydney are greeted by a fascinating structure out in the harbour. With its sail-like roof, the Sydney Opera House stands gleaming in the sunlight, a true marvel of the modern world. Construction of the foundation and base took four years, from 1959 to 1963. Next came the creation of the roof. Made from over 2000 prefabricated sections, it is held together by 347 km of cable. The roof shells are covered with ceramic tiles that sparkle in the sunlight. In 1973, the Opera House was officially opened. Over fifty million people have visited Sydney's wonder in the harbour.

7. The Canadian Museum of Civilization

The curved stone walls of the Canadian Museum of Civilization flow like melting glaciers and reflect the windswept rocks of Canada's landscape. It's no accident: Douglas Cardinal, a First Nations architect from Alberta, designed the museum to look like the landforms of Canada. The museum opened in 1989 in Hull, Québec, across the river from Parliament Hill in Ottawa. Inside, interactive exhibits and "live" displays bring thousands of years of Canadian history to life and celebrate the creative genius of all people.

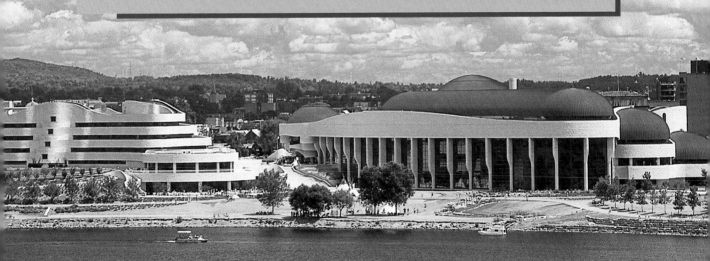

Which of the wonders of the world do you like best? Can you add any of your own favourite wonders to the article?

Make a Mural of Wonders

Working in a small group, decide how you would create a mural to display the wonders of the world. Among your choices are

✎ a world map showing where the wonders are located

✎ a time line showing when the wonders were built

Be sure to use illustrations and captions, and to give your mural a big title.

Understanding the Article

How Marvellous!

- Review the *Seven Wonders of the Ancient World*. In your opinion, which one is (a) the biggest (b) the most beautiful (c) the most unusual?

- What kinds of disasters destroyed many of the ancient wonders? Do these disasters still occur today?

- Skim *Seven Marvels You Can Visit Today*. In your opinion, which is (a) the most surprising (b) the most mysterious (c) the most beautiful (d) the hardest to visit?

- How many of the ancient and modern wonders were built for the glory of one powerful person or family?

- If you could build one of the wonders in your community, which one would you choose? Why?

YOUR TURN TO WRITE

A Story

Any of the wonders of the world could be the setting for a marvellous story. What if a ship lost at sea saw the light of the Pharos of Alexandria? What if a detective solved the mystery of the Easter Island statues? What if the Sydney Opera House had a phantom backstage? Pick your wonder and tell your most imaginative story!

Report on Natural Wonders

The wonders of nature are just as marvellous as the built wonders in our article. On our continent, there are Niagara Falls, the Grand Canyon, and the Rocky Mountains—to name just a few. With the help of your librarian, choose seven wonders of the natural world. Prepare an illustrated poster with pictures and captions (your captions should explain why your wonder is so wonderful!)

Glacier, Yukon Territory

Badlands, Alberta

Lush, old-growth forest, British Columbia

Three Marvellous Careers

Each of the following three paragraphs describes a career. Which of these careers do you think you would enjoy?

1. There wouldn't be any wonders of the world without architects. For this career, you need artistic talent, an interest in how people live and work, and the ability to turn drawings into structures.

2. There wouldn't be any written records of how and why marvels were built without historians. For this career, you need an interest in the past, a love of reading and research, and a talent for writing.

3. After marvels have fallen into ruins, we wouldn't know much about them without archaeologists. For this career, you need a knowledge of the past, patience in looking for things, and skill in organizing and interpreting what you find.

**BEFORE
READING**

What do you know about cave people? Where did they live? What did they eat and wear? Did they have medicines? What did they do in their spare time? List your ideas in your notebook.

The Painted Caves of Altamira

Historical Account adapted from
CANADIAN CHILDREN'S ANNUAL

Illustrations by
LÁSZLÓ GÁL

In the mid-nineteenth century, people knew very little about our ancient ancestors, the cave dwellers. However, scientists and archaeologists were eagerly studying prehistory. They wanted to learn all about those thousands of years before written history—when the earliest human beings appeared on earth. No one expected a twelve-year-old girl to make an important discovery...

1868, near the village of Santillana del Mar, in northern Spain

A farmer hunting for foxes loses his dog on the hillside. Then he hears a faint whining and barking. Apparently, the dog has followed a fox into a hole, and now it can't get out. The farmer kneels down and starts clearing the rocks.

"Hold on, you silly dog. I'll have you out in a minute," he calls.

Finally the hole is big enough for the farmer to get his head and shoulders through. Reaching down, he pulls the dog out by the scruff of its neck. Now he's curious. Could this be a cave? He lowers himself through the hole. There is enough light to show him that he really is in a cave—the first one ever found here on Altamira, and a very large one.

The farmer hurries back to his village to tell of his discovery. But no one seems very interested.

1875, the nearby estate of Don Marcelino de Sautuola

Seven years later, an employee on Don Marcelino's estate hears about the cave and tells his employer. He knows that the Don, an engineer, is interested in geology—the study of rocks—and prehistory.

Don Marcelino immediately rides over to Altamira with two workers. They enlarge the entrance to the cave and go inside. While he is digging, Don Marcelino notices animal bones—all split in half lengthwise—and stones fashioned like the tools he has seen in museums.

He believes this must be the cave dwelling of prehistoric people. Gathering several of the bones and stone tools, he goes to visit a friend at the university of Madrid, capital city of Spain. Don Vilanova y Piera, a professor of geology, confirms his friend's idea that the cave was a prehistoric dwelling.

"These bones were split by cave dwellers to get at the marrow—very nutritious," Don Vilanova says.

"And the stone tools?"

"From the early Stone Age period, called the Paleolithic Age," the professor explains.

Thrilled, Don Marcelino reveals that he wants to excavate the cave. But his friend suggests that he study other prehistoric sites and museums before going back to dig. For four years, Don Marcelino follows his advice.

Based on the article, add to your list of facts about cave people. What are you still curious about? Write five questions you would like to find answers for.

IMAGINE!

Like Maria, you make a great discovery, right in your own neighbourhood! Write a short report about it for your local newspaper.

Understanding the Selection

Maria's Discovery

- Why do you think people (then and now) are interested in prehistory?

- The cave paintings at Altamira were discovered almost by accident. Tell the story in your own words.

- In your opinion, what was the most marvellous thing about the paintings in Altamira?

- Why do you think the first people to hear about the paintings dismissed them as fakes?

- What are cave paintings all about? Which explanation makes the most sense to you?

Cave People in the Media

Media Link

Make a list of movies, cartoons, television shows, and comic strips about the earliest humans. Which are the most enjoyable? Which ones are the silliest? Which ones give the most reliable information about cave people?

Movies pictured are *Caveman* (top); *The Flintstones* (middle); *The History of the World: Part 1* (bottom).

Make Your Own Rock Art

1. Begin by finding a few large rocks. Run your hands over the surface. Can you feel an animal emerging from the rock? Think about what you might paint.

2. Collect charcoal pencils and three colours of paint. Decide if you want to paint with a brush or use your fingers (the artist at Altamira may have done both).

3. Sketch your animal with charcoal, then fill in the outline with paint. Use the bumps and hollows in the stone to give the animal a solid, muscular feel.

Did You Know ?

A petroglyph is a figure carved into a rockface, usually near water. They have been found everywhere in the world. Across Canada, First Nations people etched mysterious petroglyphs on rocks and cliffs. You can see them in Petroglyph Park in Nanaimo, B.C., Writing-On-Stone Provincial Park in southern Alberta, and Petroglyph Provincial Park near Peterborough, Ontario.

A petroglyph of a fish found at Petroglyph Park, Vancouver Island, BC.

Words in Context

Write your own definitions for these terms. First, use the context clues in the article (nearby phrases that explain the terms). If you need more help, look them up in your dictionary.

prehistory	Paleolithic Age
geologist	excavate
archaeologist	three-dimensional effect
Stone Age	forgeries

Fossils

POEM BY **Lilian Moore**

ILLUSTRATION BY **Chum McLeod**

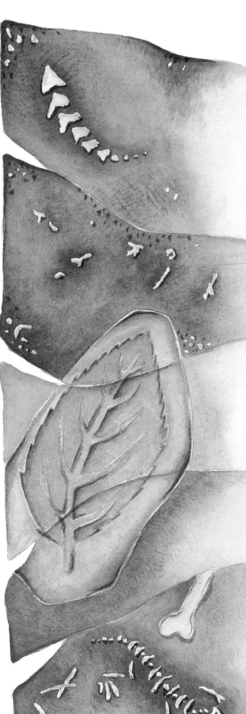

Older than
books,
than scrolls,

older
than the first
tales told

or the
first words
spoken

are the stories

in forests that
turned to
stone

in ice walls
that trapped the
mammoth

in the long
bones of
dinosaurs—

the fossil
stories that begin
Once upon a time

Personal Response

- Have you ever found a fossil, or seen one up close? If yes, how did you feel?

- How has the poet communicated her sense of wonder about fossils?

Fossil-Hunting with Lillian the Albertosaurus

As you can see, I'm a dinosaur, and I'm a tour guide at the Royal Tyrrell Museum in Drumheller, Alberta. I'm from the Cretaceous period (140-164 million years ago).

Let's start by looking at fossils and what they can tell a paleontologist. You know fossils are traces of ancient plants and animals. But did you know they hold all kinds of information?

A paleontologist can study a fossil and know how many millions of years old it is. Marks on the bone can show where the muscles were attached and how they were used. The shape of a fossilized tooth tells the scientist what kind of food the animal ate. (Meat-eaters, like myself, had long, pointed teeth that look like steak knives!)

In 1987, scientists at my museum found fossilized dinosaur eggs with unhatched dinosaurs inside. They studied these fossils to find out how fast dinosaurs grew.

Did you know that even footprints can fossilize? They're called **trackways** and they give clues as to how fast dinosaurs walked.

Paleontologists are like detectives, and each fossil is like a clue.

Write a paragraph explaining in your own words why a fossil is like a clue.

This is a true story about a schoolboy who lived in Pictou, Nova Scotia, over 150 years ago. Read on to find out why the events in this story became a turning point in young William Dawson's life.

BIOGRAPHY BY

**Joyce
Barkhouse**

Sir William Dawson

Pioneer Geologist

Squeak! Squeak!

William Dawson's slate pencil had a flaw. He looked up fearfully at the schoolmaster and met the stern gaze of cold blue eyes. He turned the pencil around and tried the other end.

Screech!

The schoolmaster couldn't stand a squeaky pencil. Thwack! The cruel rod came down across William's shoulders.

"Put your pencil down and finish your sums after school."

The room was quiet. William was a hardworking, clever, quiet boy. He had never been punished before.

He was surprised when he came out into the late afternoon sunshine to find a group of boys waiting for him.

"Hey, Willie! Come on down to the old quarry. There's a place you can get bits of slate to make perfect pencils."

For a moment William hesitated. The boys had never asked him to go anywhere with them before. His parents were strict and he was supposed to go home at once after school. He had no real friends because he could never join in their games and adventures. But he *had* to have a new pencil, and pennies were hard to come by in the Dawson home ever since his father had lost all his money during the bad days of 1834.

He piled his books with the others under a tree and soon the boys were scrambling like chipmunks along the steep bank of the stone quarry. The sandstone was crumbly and the flakes of shale pried out easily with a pocket knife. William dug away and then suddenly stopped and stared with astonishment at what he held in his hand.

The boy nearest him looked up to see a strange expression on William's face.

"Hey! What is it, Willie? What'cha got?"

But William closed his hand over his find.

"Hey! Fellows! Willie's found something! Maybe he's struck gold!"

Gold! The word was magic to the poor children of the struggling pioneers of Pictou town. They came tumbling and scrambling from all directions to surround William Dawson.

"Let's see. Let's see it, Willie."

He opened his hand and showed them what he had found.

It was not gold. There was a long silence. Then one of the boys snorted in disgust.

"What's so wonderful?" he asked, scornfully.

"Look! Look at the leaf! It's like an artist made it!" cried William. His voice trembled with excitement.

"So? Do you cry when you wake up in winter and see frostleaves on your window pane?"

All the boys hooted, and burst out laughing.

"The lad's loony!"

"Willie's got bats in his belfry!"

How could somebody get so excited over a little piece of ordinary rock with some broken tracings on it? They ran off and left him. He really must be crazy, that one.

William hardly realized the boys had gone. He was fascinated by the picture of the leaf in the rock. It was rather like a fern but different from any he had seen before. How had it come there, buried so deep in the rock? Could there be any more?

He opened his pocket handkerchief and laid the flake of rock on it carefully. He had forgotten all about slate pencils. He began to dig again. Not only did he find more stone leaves, but he found something that looked like the shape of a weird bug.

When he got home his mother was waiting at the door. Before she had a chance to scold him for being so late, he opened his handkerchief and showed her his treasures.

She examined them, glancing with understanding at her son's flushed face.

"Yes, it's an interesting find. I've heard of such things being discovered in collieries back home in Scotland," she said.

"But what does it mean? How can these stone leaves and bugs lie buried in the cliffs?"

"Why, that I canna tell you, laddie. But look at you! Face and shirt all covered with dirt. Get some water in the basin and wash up. When your father gets home perhaps he'll be able to explain it to you."

William felt sure his father would know the answer, but Mr. Dawson was away several days before the boy had a chance to show him the little collection of rocks carefully arranged on the shelves of a cupboard in his bedroom.

"Now this reminds me of a very strange thing," exclaimed his father. "You recall me telling you about the long journey my friends and I made afoot when we determined to leave Scotland for Nova Scotia? Well, when we were high in the Grampian Hills we came upon a quarry dug deep into the side of a mountain. Farmers came up there to dig and to cart back loads of the fine loose soil to use as fertilizer. When we examined this rich soil we found it to be made of shells. A whole mountain of finely crushed seashells!"

William stared at his father wonderingly.

"But how did those shells get there?"

His father shook his head.

"It's a great mystery."

He pulled his beard in bewilderment.

"But I want to know! I must find out!" cried William.

Mr. Dawson gave his son a hard look. He demanded absolute respect from his children. Then his expression softened. It was he, himself, who had taught this child the love of truth and the quest for knowledge. He said, "There is one man who may be able to give you an answer. That's Dr. McCullough, the principal of Pictou Academy."

William's eyes widened. Dr. McCullough! Would that great and learned man waste his time answering a schoolboy's questions?

He went to school as usual the next day and had to endure the taunts of the other boys at recess.

"Willie's got rocks in his head!"

"Ha, ha, Willie! Found any more pictures in the rocks?"

William felt the hot blood burn in his cheeks, but he did not answer back. He had permission from his father to walk over to Pictou Academy after school to ask a question of Dr. McCullough.

His heart was pounding when he knocked at the door of the principal's office.

Dr. McCullough looked up from his desk in some astonishment at the pale, shy boy who had dared to enter his presence.

"Yes?" he enquired, shortly.

William pulled off his cap and bowed.

"Please, sir, I found these over in the quarry and I'd like to know what they are and how they got there."

Dr. McCullough opened the handkerchief and spread the contents on his desk. He pulled out a magnifying glass and studied each one intently. William Dawson waited, his heart thumping against his ribs. Finally the great man spoke.

"Why, these are fossils, and very fine specimens too. I'd like to add them to my collection here at the college. Sit down, lad, and I'll tell you all about them."

That was William Dawson's first lesson in geology. He grew up to be Sir William Dawson, one of Canada's earliest geologists. He wrote many books and papers on the subject. He also was the first Superintendent of Education in Nova Scotia, and he was knighted by Queen Victoria for his work as the "father" of McGill University in Montreal.

And what were the names of the boys who mocked young William Dawson? Nobody knows. ◈

Why was finding the fossils a turning point in William Dawson's life? Have you ever been so excited by something that you thought, "This is what I want to do with my life?"

Understanding the Selection

Bats in his Belfry

- What problems did young William have that made him an outsider at school?

- Why do you think the other boys failed to see the magic in William's fossil?

- William's father was very strict, but he helped him when it counted. What did he do?

- Do you think the ending of the story is a good one? Why?

IMAGINE!
You discover a nest of fossilized dinosaur eggs, and one of them starts to hatch! Write the story of what happens.

Something To Think About

William's father taught his children "the love of truth and the quest for knowledge." Would you teach your children the same thing? What other great lessons can a parent give a child?

A Story

William Dawson's discovery met with ridicule and indifference. But because he had a strong desire to know something, he persisted and followed his dream. Do you know someone like William who succeeded against all odds? Write your own story about that person, or invent a story that you would like to tell.

Character of a Scholar

Even as a schoolboy, William Dawson had the kind of character that makes a person a good scholar or researcher. Find examples in the story that show he had each of the characteristics at right. Add your examples to a chart in your notebook.

Characteristic	Example
curiosity	
determination	
a sense of wonder	
a need to understand	

Did You Know ?

JURASSIC BIRDS

In 1998, two fossilized animals were found in China. A group led by Philip Currie, a paleontologist from Drumheller, Alberta, studied the fossils. The animals were feathered, flightless dinosaurs that lived more than 120 million years ago! They're related to the tiny, vicious velociraptor featured in the movie *Jurassic Park.* Why was this discovery so exciting? Because these fossils provide further proof that birds evolved from small, meat-eating dinosaurs.

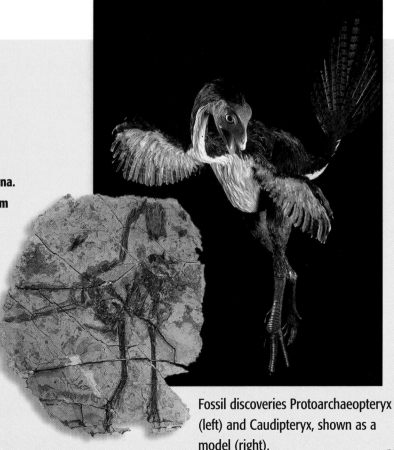

Fossil discoveries Protoarchaeopteryx (left) and Caudipteryx, shown as a model (right).

What if a 3000-year-old mummy could speak—what would it say to you? That's what author Eve Bunting asked herself before she wrote this story-poem.

Ancient Egypt: Over 4000 years ago, Egypt became the birthplace of one of the world's first civilizations.

The Nile River: This river was the heartland of Ancient Egypt. Each year it flooded and left a layer of rich, black farming soil along its banks.

The Pharaoh: The rulers of Ancient Egypt were called pharaohs.

Horus: A sky-god who was pictured as a falcon (many Egyptian gods and goddesses had animal heads or bodies).

I AM THE
Mummy
Heb-Nefert

POEM BY **Eve Bunting**   ILLUSTRATIONS BY **David Christiana**

I am the mummy Heb-Nefert,
black as night,
stretched as tight
as leather on a drum.
My arms are folded
on my hollow chest
where once my live heart beat.
My ears are holes
that hear no sound.
Once I was the daughter of a nomarch*,
favoured, beautiful.
But all things change.

---

* See Glossary on page 125.

I danced one evening for the pharaoh's brother, Ti.
My pleated linen robe
swayed gentle at my every step.
The circlet on my head
gleamed with its jewelled light.
My eyes, my hands
gave promises of bliss
that made him weak.
And soon he loved me.

I was a cherished wife.
The palace was my home.
I lived for him and he for me.

We sailed upon the Nile,
my lord and I,
the wildfowl rising from the reeds
along the bank,
the ripples of the sacred river
soft against our boat.
Sometimes we saw a hippopotamus,
great jaws agape,
a crocodile.
But we were ever safe.

We'd wander in the gardens, he and I,
beside the pleasure lake
where lotus blossoms grew.
The servant girls would come
on soundless feet
and bring us fruit—grapes, dates, and figs—
the baskets balanced on their heads,
a cloth of linen spread
beneath a canopy that kept us from the sun.
And we would feast
while harpists played.

One day, disguised,
my handmaiden and I
went back to where I once had lived
before the pharaoh's brother loved me.

I watched the women crushing wheat
to make the bread.
I saw the men hoeing the fields,
the boys beside them
using stones in slings
to scare the birds away.

I wept a little,
but I knew my life was good,
so good, beside my lord.

My golden cat, Nebut, I loved.
She loved me, too,
and came with me
into the silent twilight of the afterlife
when day changed to eternity.

I rose above myself
and watched.

I watched as they
anointed me with oils and spices,
took away the parts of me
that were inside,
and filled me up
with natron, cinnamon, and herbs.
My eyes were closed and plugged.
Beeswax filled my nose.
They capped my nails with gold
studded with precious stones,
bejewelled me from head to toe,
and bound me up in linen,
layer on layer.
I was to be
for all eternity
well kept for him.

They made a mask
painted to look like me,
bound up my cat and masked her, too,
my faithful cat, Nebut.
Placed me in my sarcophagus
pictured around with likenesses
of gods who would receive me.

The sled that took me to my tomb
was pulled by oxen.

Behind, the lines of weepers wept
and sprinkled dust about their heads
to show their grief.
Porters carried things that I would need,
the food that I would eat,
my jewels, amulets, my offerings to the gods.

Great golden Horus, Falcon in the Sky,
awaited me,
and he would greet
the barge that bore me
through the streams of stars.

I would be blessed.

They placed me gently in the tomb,
juniper berries at my head and feet,
my gilded cat, Nebut, to stay with me.

My dear lord wept.
The pharaoh said
an amulet
would bear his brother's name and mine.
The world would know
we two had loved.

My Noble One grew old
and also left that life
to lie at last beside me
in the night that followed night.
Time passed and time,
dark time and years,
till we were found,
our bodies moved,
placed in glass coffins
under lights
in quiet rooms.

I rose above myself and watched
as people came.
They peered into the cases where we lay.

They spoke,
the words unknown to me
but understood as they were said.
"This was a person? This...and this?"

How foolish that they do not see
how all things change,
and so will they.
Three thousand years from now
they will be dust and bones.
I am the mummy Heb-Nefert,
black as night,
stretched as tight
as leather on a drum.

Once I was beautiful.

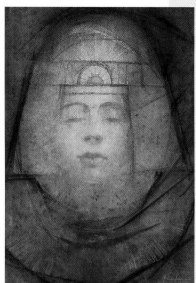

HOW

Article by
NICHOLAS REEVES
Illustrations by
JACK MCMASTER

The ancient Egyptians believed that after death their spirits would travel to another world during the day, and at night would return to their bodies. In order for a person's spirit to live forever, it had to be able to recognize and return to the body. If a spirit couldn't recognize the body it belonged to, it would die. That is why the Egyptians wanted to preserve the bodies of their dead in as lifelike a state as possible. Mummification guaranteed eternal life for the spirit.

1 After the body had been washed with wine and spices, all of the parts that might decay were removed. The embalmers first removed the brain through the nose using a long hook. Next, they made a deep cut in the abdomen and took out the internal organs: the lungs, the stomach, the liver, and the intestines.

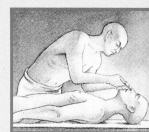

MUMMIES WERE MADE

2 The body was stuffed with bundles of a strong drying salt called natron. It was then 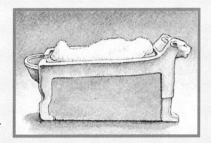 completely covered with natron and placed on a slanted embalming couch so that any fluids that dripped out as the body was drying could be collected and buried along with it.

3 While the body was drying, the internal organs were also dried and preserved with natron. They were then wrapped in strips of  linen, placed in tiny coffins, and put in a chest divided into four compartments. Each compartment had a lid with the face of a pharaoh.

4 After forty days, the body, now completely dry and shrunken, was removed from the natron. The bundles of natron were taken from inside the body cavity and the whole body was washed inside and out with oil and fragrant spices.

5 The mummy's head and body were packed with linen soaked in scented oil so that they would regain the shape they had in life. Once this was done, the mummy could be covered with necklaces, rings, and bracelets made of gold and gems.

6 The entire body was then covered in shrouds and bound with strips of linen until the mummy had returned to its original size.  This was a complicated job and could take as long as a week. Small magical objects were placed between the layers of wrapping to protect the mummy's spirit on its way to the afterworld.

7 After the wrapping was finished, the head of the mummy was covered with a portrait mask, just to  make sure that the spirit would recognize it. The masked mummy was then placed in a series of gilded wooden coffins and finally put into a sarcophagus.

FOLLOW UP

How do you feel about the mummy's story? Does Heb-Nefert seem like a real, live person to you? What are some of the details the author puts in her story that bring the mummy back to life?

Understanding the Poem

All Things Change

- What are some of the pleasures Heb-Nefert enjoyed when she was alive? What made her sad?

- What do you think she means when she says, "I rose above myself / and watched"?

- After thousands of years, the two mummies were found and moved. How do you think this happened?

- What does Heb-Nefert think about the people who come to see her in the museum?

- Compare the steps in *How Mummies Were Made* with the description in the poem on pages 120-121.

Something To Think About

Near the end of the poem, Heb-Nefert says,

"How foolish that they do not see how all things change, and so will they."

Is this the message of the poem? How would you explain this message?

A Poem from the Past

Eve Bunting wrote her story from the point of view of a mummy, using the pronouns "I" and "we" to tell her tale. You can do the same thing. Visit your local museum and choose a person or object from the past that interests you. Do some research to find out more about your choice. Then tell an exciting story from the point of view of that person or object.

Glossary

amulet: a charm worn around the neck to protect a person from bad luck

circlet: a circular ornament, like a tiara

embalm: to preserve a dead body from decay

gilded: covered with a thin layer of gold

nomarch: the chief magistrate (judge) of a province of Ancient Egypt

sarcophagus: a stone coffin ornamented with sculpture or inscriptions

shroud: a cloth used to wrap a body for burial

Find Out About...

Treasures of the Tombs

The tombs of Egyptian kings and queens were packed with treasures. Most of the riches were soon carted off by robbers, but one tomb was overlooked—the tomb of the boy-king Tutankhamen, who died when he was about eighteen years old. When the tomb was finally discovered in 1922, by British archaeologist Howard Carter, it became a new wonder of the world. More than 5000 objects were found in its four rooms, many of them gold. King Tut's portrait mask is one of the most famous faces of the ancient world.

Prepare a report on the treasures of the Egyptian tombs. Present your findings in a container the shape of a pyramid!

TECH LINK
Use multimedia software to create an interactive presentation.

Treasures from King Tutankhamen's tomb.

125

Article by **SHELLEY TANAKA**

Have you ever heard of a natural mummy? That's the body of a person or animal that has been preserved by a natural process, rather than by embalming. Read the article to find out how this can happen!

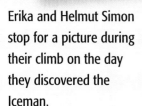

Erika and Helmut Simon stop for a picture during their climb on the day they discovered the Iceman.

THE DISCOVERY

Erika and Helmut Simon loved to climb the snow-covered Alps between Austria and Italy. On September 19, 1991, they reached the summit of a peak called Finailspitze just before noon. On their way back down, they left the marked path and crossed a glacier. That's when they saw it.

It looked like a doll at first—a bare, brown head and bony shoulders sticking out of a slushy puddle of melting snow.

The Simons drew nearer. They bent down for a closer look. "It's a man!" cried Erika.

Two days later, on September 21, archaeologist Konrad Spindler was getting ready for a new term of teaching and research at the University of Innsbruck in Austria. He was reading the local newspaper when he spotted a short item. Two tourists had found a body sticking out of a glacier in the Alps. The police had been called. They thought the corpse might belong to a mountain climber who had died in an accident, maybe several decades ago.

Spindler paid little attention. The body of a modern-day mountain climber didn't much interest an archaeologist who specialized in ancient things. Besides, about two hundred hikers died in the Alps every year from rockslides, avalanches, crevasses, sudden fogs, or snow squalls. The death of yet another was sad, but it was not unusual.

So he was surprised to see that the body was still in the news a few days later. People had started to notice some odd things about this particular corpse. There were peculiar marks on the man's back. There was a big clump of straw on his foot, covered with torn pieces of leather. Strange tools lay scattered around him. A squashed birchbark tube had been found nearby.

And there were more mysteries. The body didn't look like the corpses that normally emerged from the glacier. It hadn't been crushed and torn apart by the grinding force of the ice. Its skin wasn't white and waxy but brown and shrivelled like that of a mummy. It appeared to be quite old.

THE INVESTIGATION

Early in the morning of September 24, the phone rang in Spindler's office. It was the university's forensic* department.

Spindler learned that air-rescue operators and mountaineers had been hacking at the body for several days. Finally they were able to pull it out of the ice. It had been wrapped in a plastic bag, stuffed into a coffin, and taken to the nearest medical lab. At that very moment, it lay on a stainless-steel table—in a building that was only minutes away from Spindler's office. Would he like to see it?

---

*forensic: the application of medical and other science to police work.

A helicopter transports the Iceman to a nearby town (top) where he is placed in a coffin (bottom).

Rescue workers chip away at the ice surrounding the Iceman.

It was very quiet and cool in the laboratory. The room smelled like a hospital. The forensic experts led Spindler to a dissecting table covered with a sheet. A clock ticked softly.

Spindler would remember this precise moment for the rest of his life.

The sheet was pulled away. And there lay the shrivelled, naked body of a man.

His nose was squashed. His mouth was gaping. His eyelids were open, and sunken eyeballs gazed out of their sockets. His left hip had been torn open by a jackhammer that had been used to try to free him from the ice.

But what interested Spindler the most were the things that lay beside the body—the objects that had been found with the man. There was a long piece of wood that had been broken off at one end. There was a smooth, flat white bead attached to a fringe of tassels. There was a pouch with a stone knife sticking out of it.

And there was an axe. It was small but well made. The handle had been carefully carved and shaped. The blade had been bound into the wood with leather straps.

Spindler's mind raced. He had seen axes like this before. He knew that such tools had been made only a very, very long time ago.

This was not the body of a mountain climber who had been dead for several decades. In fact, Konrad Spindler knew immediately that this man had died at least 4000 years ago!

THE DISCOVERY SITE

Many of the Iceman's belongings were found near his body. Pictured here are some of these artifacts as they would have looked during his life. Other remains included fragments of clothing and pieces of a wooden backpack frame.

FUR HAT
Archaeologists found a fur hat during their second visit to the site in August 1992. It lay 70 cm from where the mummy's head had been.

QUIVER
A long fur sack made of deerskin, stiffened by a wooden rod, held the Iceman's fourteen arrows. Two of them were ready to use, with flint arrowheads still in place.

AXE
The metal blade and shape of the axe head gave Konrad Spindler the first clue that the Iceman's body was at least 4000 years old.

BIRCHBARK CONTAINERS
Pieces of two birchbark containers were found at the site; one of them had held embers for starting a fire.

BOW
The Iceman had carefully placed his unfinished bow against a rock. It was broken in two during the recovery effort. The lower end of the bow was found stuck in the ice in August 1992.

DAGGER
The Iceman carried a small dagger with a flint blade and a scabbard.

SHOE
The Iceman's shoes were made from cowhide.

Knotted grass cords formed a netting around the heel. The shoes were stuffed with grass for warmth.

1. About 5300 years ago, the Iceman died in a narrow hollow in the mountains. Most likely a cold, dry snow began to fall shortly afterward, freeze-drying the body.

2. Over hundreds of years, more and more snow fell. Eventually a glacier moved over the rocks, but the Iceman's frozen body remained protected in the hollow underneath.

WHO WAS THE ICEMAN?

The Iceman's axe gave archaeologist Konrad Spindler the first clue that the body was extremely old. But determining the body's exact age was a long, delicate job that involved many scientists and scholars.

Experts identified the metal in the man's axe. They X-rayed his equipment. They tested his skin and bones and the grass found with him by a method known as **carbon-14 dating**.

WHAT IS CARBON-14 DATING?

Archaeologists use carbon-14 dating to find out how old the remains of a plant, animal, or human are. Living things are made up of millions of tiny particles called atoms, and some of these atoms are of a special kind called **carbon 14**. When a living thing dies, most of the atoms remain, but the carbon-14 atoms slowly begin to break down. By counting how many carbon-14 atoms were left in small pieces of the Iceman's bone and tissue, and in grass blades from his cape, scientists could tell that he died about 5300 years ago.

Then all the tests were performed again, and the results were compared with those done by other scientists. Finally there was no doubt. The body was even older than Konrad Spindler had guessed. The Iceman was 5300 years old—his was the oldest human body that had ever been found so well preserved.

3. Slowly the glacier began to melt. In 1991, desert storms in North Africa blew clouds of dust over the Alps. The dark dust absorbed the heat of the sun, causing the ice to melt more quickly.

4. In September 1991, Erika and Helmut Simon spotted the Iceman's head in the melting snow. Scientists believe the body had been uncovered for just three days before the discovery.

The Iceman lived during the late Stone Age. He died five hundred years before the Egyptians built the first pyramids.

For the archaeologists, the real work was just beginning. There were hundreds of questions that needed to be answered. Who was the Iceman? What were all his tools and equipment used for? What was he doing so high up on the mountain, and how did he die? Why was his body so well preserved? Some of these questions have been answered, but many mysteries remain.

Nobody knows for certain where the Iceman came from, or exactly how he died. He could have been a shepherd who was caught in a sudden snowstorm while bringing his herd down the mountain. He could have been hunting animals or looking for precious metals on the rocky mountain slopes. He could have been fleeing an enemy attack on his village, or just on his way to visit friends in a hilltop village.

Archaeologist Konrad Spindler (left) and other experts at the University of Innsbruck examine the Iceman.

When we look at photographs of the Iceman, we see a shrivelled, naked body and a battered, sunken face. But that body and face belonged to a real human being. They belonged to a man who lived in a world that was probably inhabited by people just like him—people who were in many ways not so different from ourselves. ◈

FOLLOW UP

Why was it so exciting to find the Iceman in mummy form, instead of just finding his bones?

Understanding the Article

A Freeze-Dried Body

- What clues convinced people that the body was older than they thought?

- How did Konrad Spindler, the archaeologist, know that the man had died at least 4000 years ago?

- Do you think the Iceman was similar to people living today, or very different? Why?

IMAGINE!
You are an expert in carbon-14 dating. Something mysterious has been found and you must determine how old it is. What is it and why is it important?

YOUR TURN TO WRITE

A Story

The article tells you quite a lot about the Iceman: where he was found, what he was wearing, what he was carrying with him, and why his body was so well preserved. But there are hundreds of questions that still need to be answered. Who was the Iceman? Did he have a family? What were all his tools and equipment used for? What was he doing so high up on the mountain? How did he die? The archaeologists are still trying to answer these questions.

Think about the facts you know, then make up your own story to answer the questions. Give it the usual story elements—an interesting opening sentence, a problem for the Iceman to solve, suspense as he tries to solve it, and a satisfying ending.

Did You Know ?

What was happening around the world when the Iceman lived in 3300 B.C.?

Middle East:
The first cities develop in Sumer (now Iraq).

Africa:
The Egyptians develop a way of writing called hieroglyphics.

Europe:
People raise huge standing stones like the ones at Stonehenge.

China:
Longshan people craft fine black ceramics.

3500-2500 B.C.

Americas:
Mexican cave dwellers farm maize (a kind of corn).

India:
Villages grow in the fertile Indus Valley.

MORE GOOD READING

Marvels Then and Now

🍁 **I Was There series**
by Shelley Tanaka
– *Discovering the Iceman*
– *The Buried City of Pompeii*
– *On Board the Titanic*

This series of books is filled with amazing facts, photos, and illustrations about some of the wondrous events in our history: the discovery of a 5300-year-old mummy, the sinking of the Titanic, and the explosion of the volcano Vesuvius that destroyed the city of Pompeii. (information books)

Talking Walls
by Margy Burns Knight

If the most famous walls in the world could talk, what would they tell us? This book gives you a chance to see different cultures by exploring walls around the world, including the Great Wall of China and the Western Wall in Jerusalem. (a picture book)

🍁 *Trapped in Ice*
by Eric Walters

In 1913, Captain Robert Bartlett leads an expedition to the Arctic. On that journey are thirteen-year-old Helen and her brother Michael. In her diary, Helen records what happens to the crew and her family when the Arctic Ocean freezes early and they are forced to make their way over land. Based on true events. (a novel)

Fantastic Fiction

Fantastic Fiction:

stories that tell of imaginary magical creatures (like elves, giants, or leprechauns) in ordinary everyday settings, or in magical lands (like Oz, Narnia, or Wonderland). This genre also includes stories of incredible or magical events that happen to ordinary people.

Preview this selection by reading the book titles and looking quickly at the art. How do you think these stories fit the definition of fantastic fiction on page 135?

Fantastic Books!

All kinds of fantasy stories are waiting for you in your nearest library. Most of these books have fantastic art, too! Just like the stories, the illustrations stretch the imagination and boggle the mind!

Would you like to have tea with the Mad Hatter, or play croquet with the Queen of Hearts? In *Alice's Adventures in Wonderland* by Lewis Carroll, Alice does just that, and has many other amazing adventures.

◄ Some houses have bats and some have mice, but some homes have *Borrowers*! Author Mary Norton has written several fanciful books about these tiny folk that live within our walls and borrow whatever they need.

BORROWERS
MARY NORTON
ILLUSTRATED BY BETH AND JOE KRUSH

What happens when a man is shipwrecked on a strange island? In *Gulliver in Lilliput,* the hero wakes up to find he's a giant, pinned to the ground by the little people of Lilliput. Margaret Hodges has retold Jonathan Swift's 280-year-old story for modern kids to enjoy.

For young Jakkin, finding a dragon to train is his only hope for freedom. Find out what happens when he gets that dragon in *Dragon's Blood* by Jane Yolen, the first book in a series.

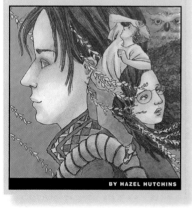

Have you ever liked a character in a book so much that you wished the person could come to life? That's what happens in *The Prince of Tarn* by Hazel Hutchins—a character from a book comes to life. Fred and Rebecca have an unbelievable adventure with the prince, and learn what it means to be heroes.

Have you ever dreamed of flying, or wished that you could stay young forever? *Peter Pan* by J.M. Barrie is a fantastic story about a land where children can do both—Neverland. But watch out for Captain Hook!

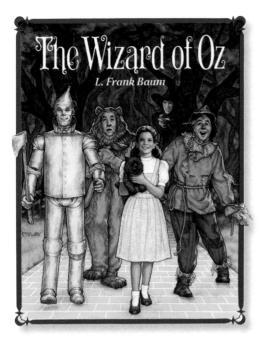

Some people lose their homes during a tornado; Dorothy lost her world—and found herself in the land of Oz! Oz is an amazing place where Dorothy, a cowardly lion, a brainless scarecrow, and a heartless tinman help each other get what they truly desire.

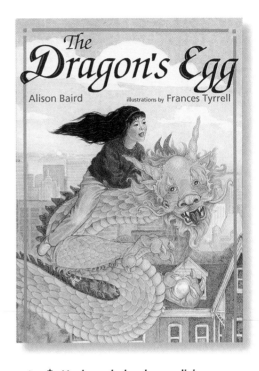

Having a baby dragon living with you can be fun—until it starts to grow! In *The Dragon's Egg* by Alison Baird, a young girl from Toronto's Chinatown, Ai Lien, discovers the pleasures, and headaches, of living with a dragon.

In the book *The Lion, the Witch, and the Wardrobe*, four children playing hide-and-seek discover the wonderful world of Narnia, where magic rules and good overcomes evil. This is just one of seven books about Narnia by C. S. Lewis.

RESPONDING

to FANTASTIC BOOKS!

Which of these fantasy books have you read? What do you think makes them great stories? Can you add any favourite fantasies to the list?

Personal Response

With a partner, discuss the fantasy illustrations in the selection. Which one piece of art do you think is the most imaginative? Which one makes you want to read the book? Choose your favourite pieces, and explain why you like them.

Create Fantastic Art

Begin by collecting more examples of fantastic art. Ask your school librarian for suggestions. With four or five classmates, discuss the fantasy elements in the artwork. Which illustrations inspire your imagination the most?

Now, get out your paints (or markers, or pencil crayons) and create some artwork for your favourite fantastic story. Share your art, and the story, with your group.

Book Club

GROUP DISCUSSION

Choose one of these fantastic books to read. When you've finished, hold a book talk with other students who chose the same book. Read out loud your favourite parts of the book. Discuss what makes the story a fantasy: strange creatures, unusual happenings, an invented world, or all of these. Decide who else would enjoy reading this book. Then write a short recommendation for them explaining why.

BEFORE READING

Do you know any stories—like *Aladdin and His Magic Lamp*—about a genie who offers someone a wish? With a partner, make a list of the things the characters wished for. Why do wishers often get more than they bargained for?

Fantasy Story
by
Charles de Lint

Photographs
by
Ron Tanaka

A Wish Named *Arnold*

Marguerite kept a wish in a brass egg, and its name was Arnold.

The egg screwed apart in the middle. Inside, wrapped in a small piece of faded velvet, was the wish. It was a small wish, about the length of a man's thumb, and was made of black clay in the rough shape of a bird. Marguerite decided straight away that it was a crow, even if it did have a splash of white on its head. That made it just more special for her, because she'd dyed a forelock of her own dark hair a peroxide white just before the summer started—much to her parents' dismay.

She'd found the egg under a pile of junk in Miller's while tagging along with her mother and aunt on their usual weekend tour of the local antique shops. Miller's was near their cottage on Otty Lake, just down the road from Rideau Ferry, and considered to be the best antique shop in the area.

The egg and its dubious contents were only two dollars, and maybe the egg was dinged up a little and didn't screw together quite right, and maybe the carving didn't look so much like a crow as it did a lump of black clay with what could be a beak on it, but she'd bought it all the same.

It wasn't until Arnold talked to her that she found out he was a wish.

"What do you mean, you're a wish?" she'd asked, keeping her voice low so that her parents wouldn't think she'd taken to talking in her sleep. "Like a genie in a lamp?"

Something like that.

It was all quite confusing. Arnold lay in her hand, an unmoving lump that was definitely not alive even if he did look like a bird, sort of. That was a plain fact, as her father liked to say. On the other hand, someone was definitely speaking to her in a low, buzzing voice that tickled pleasantly inside her head.

I wonder if I'm dreaming, she thought.

She gave her white forelock a tug, then brushed it away from her brow and bent down to give the clay bird a closer look.

"What sort of a wish can you give me?" she asked finally.

Think of something—any one thing that you want—and I'll give it to you.

"Anything?"

Within reasonable limits.

Marguerite nodded sagely. She was all too familiar with *that* expression. "Reasonable limits" was why she only had one forelock dyed instead of a whole swath of rainbow colours like her friend Tina, or a Mohawk like Sheila. If she just washed her hair and let it dry, *and* you ignored the dyed forelock, she had a most reasonable short haircut. But all it took was a little gel that she kept hidden in her purse, and by the time she joined her friends down at the mall, her hair was sticking out around her head in a bristle of spikes. It was just such a pain wearing a hat when she came home and having to wash out the gel right away.

Maybe that should be her wish. That she could go around looking just however she pleased and nobody could tell her any different. Except that seemed like a waste of a wish. She should probably ask for great heaps of money and jewels. Or maybe for a hundred more wishes.

"How come I only get one wish?" she asked.

Because that's all I am, Arnold replied. *One small wish.*

"Genies and magic fish give three. In fact, *everybody* in *all* the stories gets three. Isn't it a tradition or something?"

Not where I come from.

"Where *do* you come from?"

There was a moment's pause, then Arnold said softly, *I'm not really sure.*

Marguerite felt a little uncomfortable at that. The voice tickling her mind sounded too sad, and she started to feel ashamed of being so greedy.

"Listen," she said. "I didn't really mean to...you know..."

That's all right, Arnold replied. *Just let me know when you've decided what your wish is.*

Marguerite got a feeling in her head as though something had just slipped away, like a lost memory or a half-remembered thought; then she realized that Arnold had just gone back to wherever it was that he'd been before she'd opened the egg. Thoughtfully she wrapped him up in the faded velvet, then shut him away in the egg. She put the egg under her pillow and went to sleep.

All the next day she kept thinking about the brass egg and the clay crow inside it, about her one wish and all the wonderful things that there were to wish for. She meant to take out the egg right away, first thing in the morning, but she never quite found the time. She went fishing with her father after breakfast, and then she went into Perth to shop with her mother, and then she went swimming with Steve, who lived two cottages down and liked punk music as much as she did, though maybe for different reasons. She didn't get back to her egg until bedtime that night.

"What happens to you after I've made my wish?" she asked after she'd taken Arnold out of his egg.

I go away.

Marguerite asked, "Where to?" before she really thought about what she was saying, but this time Arnold didn't get upset.

To be somebody else's wish, he said.

"And after that?"

Well, after they've made their wish, I'll go on to the next, and the next...

"It sounds kind of boring."

Oh, no. I get to meet all sorts of interesting people.

Marguerite scratched her nose. She'd gotten a mosquito bite right on the end of it and felt very much like Pinocchio, though she hadn't been telling any lies.

"Have you always been a wish?" she asked, not thinking again.

Arnold's voice grew so quiet that it was just a feathery touch in her mind. *I remember being something else...a long time ago...*

Marguerite leaned closer, as though that would help her hear him better. But there was a sudden feeling in her as though Arnold had shaken himself out of his reverie.

Do you know what you're going to wish for yet? he asked briskly.

"Not exactly."

Well, just let me know when you're ready, he said, and then he was gone again.

Marguerite sighed and put him away. This didn't seem to be at all the way this whole wishing business should go. Instead of feeling all excited about being able to ask for any one thing— *anything!*—she felt guilty because she kept making Arnold feel bad. Mind you, she thought, he did seem to be a gloomy sort of a genie when you came right down to it.

She fell asleep wondering if he looked the same in whatever place he went to when he left her as he did when she held him in her hand. Somehow his ticklish, raspy voice didn't quite go with the lumpy clay figure that lay inside the brass egg. She supposed she'd never know.

As the summer progressed they become quite good friends, in an odd sort of way. Marguerite took to carrying the egg around with her in a small, quilted, cotton bag that she slung over her shoulder. At opportune moments, she'd take Arnold out and they'd talk about all sorts of things.

Arnold, Marguerite discovered, knew a lot that she hadn't supposed a genie would know. He was up on all the latest bands, seemed to have seen all the best movies, knew stories that could make her giggle uncontrollably or shiver with chills under her blankets late at night. If she didn't press him for information about his past, he proved to be the best friend a person could want, and she found herself telling him things that she'd never think of telling anyone else.

It got to the point where Marguerite forgot he was a wish. Which was fine until the day she left her quilted cotton bag behind in a restaurant in Smith Falls on a day's outing with her mother. She became totally panic-stricken until her mother took her back to the restaurant, but by then her bag was gone, and so was the egg, and with it, Arnold.

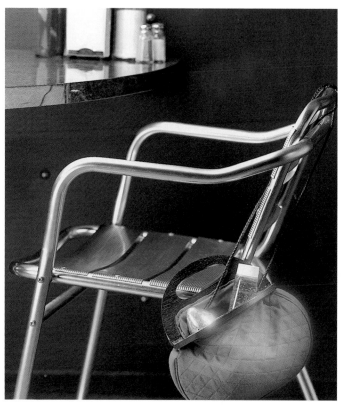

Marguerite was inconsolable. She moped around for days, and nothing that anyone could do could cheer her up. She missed Arnold passionately. Missed their long talks when she was supposed to be sleeping. Missed the weight of his egg in her shoulder bag and the companionable presence of just knowing he was there. And also, she realized, she'd missed her chance of using her wish.

She could have had anything she wanted. She could have asked for piles of money. For fame and fortune. To be a lead singer in a band like 10 000 Maniacs. To be another Molly Ringwald and star in all kinds of movies. She could have wished that Arnold would stay with her forever. Instead, jerk that she was, she'd never used the wish, and now she had nothing. How could she be so stupid?

"Oh," she muttered one night in her bed. "I wish I...I wish..."

She paused then, feeling a familiar tickle in her head.

Did you finally decide on your wish? Arnold asked.

Marguerite sat up so suddenly that she knocked over her water glass on the night table. Luckily it was empty.

"Arnold?" she asked, looking around. "Are you here?"

Well, not exactly here, as it were, but I can hear you.

"Where have you *been?*"

Waiting for you to make your wish.

"I've really missed you," Marguerite said. She patted her comforter with eager hands, trying to find Arnold's egg. "How did you get back here?"

I'm not exactly here, Arnold said.

"How come you never talked to me, when I've been missing you all this time?"

I can't really initiate these things, Arnold explained. *It gets rather complicated, but even though my egg's with someone else, I can't really be their wish until I've finished being yours.*

"So we can still talk and be friends even though I've lost the egg?"

Not exactly. I can fulfil your wish, but since I'm not with you, as it were, I can't really stay unless you're ready to make your wish.

"You can't?" Marguerite wailed.

Afraid not. I don't make the rules, you know.

"I've got it," Marguerite said. And she did have it, too. If she wanted to keep Arnold with her, all she had to do was wish for him to always be her friend. Then no one could take him away from her. They'd always be together.

"I wish..." she began.

But that didn't seem quite right, she realized. She gave her dyed forelock a nervous tug. It wasn't right to *make* someone be your friend. But if she didn't do that, if she wished something else, then Arnold would just go off and be somebody else's wish. Oh, if only things didn't have to be complicated. Maybe she should just wish herself to the moon and be done with all her problems. She could lie there and stare at the world from a nice, long distance away. That would solve everything.

She felt that telltale feeling in her mind that let her know that Arnold was leaving again.

"Wait," she said. "I haven't made my wish yet."

The feeling stopped. *Then you've decided?* Arnold asked.

She hadn't, but as soon as he asked, she realized that there was only one fair wish she could make.

"I wish you were free," she said.

The feeling that was Arnold moved blurrily inside her. *You what?* he asked.

"I wish you were free. I *can* wish that, can't I?"

Yes, but...wouldn't you rather have something...well, something for yourself?

"This *is* for myself," Marguerite said. "Your being free would be the best thing I could wish for, because you're my friend and I don't want you to be trapped anymore." She paused for a moment, brow wrinkling. "Or is there a rule against that?"

No rule, Arnold said softly. His ticklish voice bubbled with excitement. *No rule at all against it.*

"Then that's my wish," Marguerite said.

Inside her mind, she felt a sensation like a tiny whirlwind spinning around and around. It was like Arnold's voice and an autumn-leaves smell and a kaleidoscope of dervishing lights, all wrapped up in one whirling sensation.

Free! Arnold called from the centre of that whirligig. *Free free free!*

A sudden weight was in Marguerite's hand, and she saw that the brass egg had appeared there. It lay open on her palm, the faded velvet spilled out of it. It seemed so very small to hold so much happiness, but fluttering on tiny wings was the clay crow, rising up in a spin that twinned Arnold's presence in Marguerite's mind.

Her fingers closed around the brass egg as Arnold doubled, then tripled his size, in an explosion of black feathers. His voice was like a chorus of bells, ringing and ringing between Marguerite's ears. Then with an exuberant caw, he stroked the air with his wings, flew out the cottage window, and was gone.

Marguerite sat quietly, staring out of the window and holding the brass egg. A big grin stretched her lips. There was something so *right* about what she'd just done that she felt an overwhelming sense of happiness herself, as though she'd been the one trapped in a treadmill of wishes in a brass egg and Arnold had been the one to free *her*.

At last she reached out and picked up from the comforter a small, glossy, black feather that Arnold had left behind. Wrapping it in the old velvet, she put it into the brass egg and screwed the egg shut once more.

That September a new family moved in next door with a boy her age named Arnold. Marguerite was delighted, and though her parents were surprised, she and the new boy became best friends almost immediately. She showed him the egg one day that winter and wasn't at all surprised that the feather she still kept in it was the exact same shade of black as her new friend's hair.

Arnold stroked the feather with one finger when she let him see it. He smiled at her and said, "I had a wish once..."

FOLLOW UP

Is *A Wish Named Arnold* similar to, or different from, other wishing stories you've read? Do you think it had a happy ending?

Fantasy Elements

CLASS DISCUSSION

There are many different elements that work together in a good fantasy story like *A Wish Named Arnold.* Explore them in a class discussion.

- What are the magical elements in the story? (Think about strange happenings.)
- What is the emotional element? (Think about characters' feelings.)
- What is the moral element? (Think about lessons in right and wrong.)

Which of these elements is the most important? Would the story be as successful and satisfying without any one of these elements? Explain your opinion.

Understanding the Story

The Wish With a Name

- How does Arnold prove himself to be "the best friend a person could want"?

- When Arnold talks to Marguerite again after she loses him, what wish does she want to make? Why doesn't she make it?

- When Marguerite finally makes her wish, why does she feel she has made the right choice? Do you agree with her wish?

- Who do you think the boy named Arnold really is? What do you think he means when he says, "I had a wish once…"

Movies

Would *A Wish Named Arnold* make a good movie? Why or why not? Write a half-page report to a movie producer explaining

(a) why the story would make a good movie, and how you would do it

> OR

(b) why it wouldn't make a good movie in its present form, but how you would change it to make it a blockbuster

A Wish Story

Let your imagination go and write some fantastic fiction! Invent a special genie, and have her offer a wish to your main character.

As you write, think about the three elements of fantasy fiction. Also, think about how stories are structured; stories usually begin by presenting the characters, then their problem, and then the solution to the problem. Often the character changes as the story progresses.

Share the final draft of your story with your classmates, or family members.

IMAGINE!

You are a genie, and you decide to offer someone just one wish. Who will you choose? How will you make sure the person ends up happy?

BEFORE READING

The Van Gogh Café in the small town of Flowers is the setting for many magical happenings. Marc is the cook at the café, and Clara is his daughter. She's always waiting for the next story to start!

FANTASY STORY
BY
Cynthia Rylant

ILLUSTRATIONS
BY
Tomio Nitto

LIGHTNING STRIKES
at the *Van Gogh Café*

After lightning struck the Van Gogh Café one day in March, the soup didn't need to be heated for a week. You could just open up a can and the soup would be steaming.

Now it is April and the lightning is still having an effect: everything Marc cooks is coming out perfect. Perfect. Not one burnt crust, not one overcooked egg, everything has just enough salt the first time. Perfect.

The effect of this has not been lost on Marc, who has taken to writing poetry while he cooks.

Clara and Marc were both at the café when the lightning struck. In fact, they were closing up for the night. Marc had the key in the door and they were just getting ready to step out into the rain when a blinding light flashed, the café popped, and the key in Marc's hand melted inside the lock. But that was the only damage. Odd...but, of course, this is the Van Gogh Café.

Since then, things have been a little tipped, a little to one side, here at the café. The porcelain hen's smile is a bit crooked. The sign above the register won't stay straight. People come in and their hats fall off.

Clara knows it is because of the lightning. And she knows this won't last, that everything will straighten up again.

But she expects something larger to happen before everyone's hats begin staying on their heads. She expects a bigger story.

Naturally, one comes.

The smaller story began with the perfect food Marc was cooking. But this could have been just luck. Perfect food doesn't have to involve magic.

However, food that cooks itself does.

Marc is thinking of nothing else but poetry. A month ago he wasn't a poet. Now he is. He is a little crazy with writing, and since the food he's cooking has been so perfect lately, he is starting to forget it altogether. He is forgetting to flip the eggs off the grill, to pull the toast from the toaster, to change the coffee grounds.

So now the food is cooking itself.

While Marc is writing his poetry, eggs are finding the grill, frying, and flipping themselves over. Home fries are cooking up to a lovely crispness, and no matter how long they are left on the griddle, they never burn. Biscuits are showing up in pans in the oven, fluffy and hot and brushed with melted butter. Hamburgers are finding buns and lettuce, and French fries are finding oil.

Marc is writing fast, writing frantically, on anything he can find—napkins, customer bills, boxes of straws, anything. And, being the only person in the kitchen, he hasn't realized that he is not actually *cooking* all of the meals that are appearing on plates in the Van Gogh Café.

It is only when the lemon meringue pies start showing up that anyone notices what is happening. Clara notices. She realizes that her father is not the one doing the cooking, that lemon meringue pies are beyond him, and she considers saying something about it. But she is so *fond* of lemon meringue pies, and she is afraid they will disappear if she tells Marc he isn't the one who is baking them.

So she waits. She eats a lot of pie and she waits. Something else is bound to happen eventually.

And it does:

So still and blue
waiting
waiting
it is a long silver night

This is the poem Marc writes on a napkin that finds its way to Karla Roker's table. Karla

has stopped in for a piece of pie on her way to visit her boyfriend in the next town. She reads the poem on the napkin, looks puzzled, smiles. She wipes the pie off her face and heads on out to her blue truck. It is about eight, just getting dark.

And at eleven, when Karla has spent nearly two hours stranded between Flowers and the next town over because her blue truck has broken down beside Silver Lake, when she sits waiting for a tow truck to come and remembers the poem on the napkin, then the bigger story begins.

Marc's poems are telling the future.

The back of Judy Jones's bill for a grilled cheese and cola on Monday reads,

and on Tuesday her neighbour gives her a bouquet of daffodils for her birthday.

In the corner of a menu handed to Mary Showers, who has come in for lunch with her mother, a poem reads,

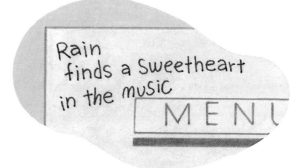

The following day, a boy in the record store asks Mary on a date.

And then the real magic happens. The magic Clara was waiting for.

One morning a young boy comes into the café. He is fighting back tears. He asks if anyone has seen his Siamese cat, who has been lost for three days.

Today is a school holiday, so Clara is working. She hasn't seen the cat, and she feels terrible for the boy. She offers him a piece of lemon meringue pie, free, and tells him she will ask the other customers about the cat while he eats.

The boy sits quietly at a table, slowly eating the pie, as Clara goes to every person in the café, hoping. But no one has seen the Siamese. They are all very sorry about it.

Clara returns to the boy and sadly shakes her head. He has finished his pie and is about to thank her and go when he glances over at the SOUP TODAY board. Under Chicken Noodle, he reads,

The boy stops in his tracks and reads the board over and over. Then he tells Clara the name of his cat: *Blackberry*. Clara tells the customer sitting at the next table and that customer tells the next and before long the whole café is looking at the soup board. Some of them have already read their futures on napkins or menus. They know what they are seeing.

The Van Gogh Café is silent. All eyes are on the board and everyone is thinking, Where is a moon-faced man in Flowers, Kansas?

Then someone whispers, "The motel." Yes.

There is only one motel in Flowers, and it is not a very good one, but it does have a lovely name that has fooled a lot of tourists who reserved their rooms sight unseen. It is called Moonlight Manor.

And its sign beside the highway shows a round, sleepy moon, eyes closed, mouth smiling, little hearts flying all around.

The motel is a good two kilometres from the café. So someone gives the boy a ride. And in the ivy planter beneath the Moonlight Manor sign, Blackberry is sleeping. Her leg has been hurt, but she is all right. The boy cries and cries; he is so happy.

The next day at the Van Gogh Café everyone is buzzing. They know for sure now that Marc's poems are omens. Fortunes. Signs. What will his next one say?

But the speculation about omens doesn't last long. It is being replaced by complaints. Frank Mills has been waiting twenty minutes for his eggs. When they finally arrive, they're runny. Kathleen Cooper's pancakes are cold. Winston Fuller's steak is tough as leather. And there's not one lemon meringue pie in sight.

Food has stopped cooking itself, Marc has stopped writing poetry, and everyone's hat is staying on his head. Things are back to normal.

Clara is naturally a little disappointed, especially about the pies. It's back to plain old apple now.

But she won't be disappointed long. Lemon meringue pies can be lovely. But they're nothing compared to magic muffins…

PERSONAL RESPONSE

If you'd like to read more stories about the Van Gogh Café, look for Cynthia Rylant's book, *The Van Gogh Cafe*, in the library.

Understanding the Story

When Lightning Strikes

- What are some of the odd effects of the lightning strike on the Van Gogh Café?

- What's special about Marc's poems?

- When does "the real magic" happen, the magic Clara was waiting for?

- Why do you think the story ended the way it did? Are you satisfied with the ending?

IMAGINE!

You eat at the Van Gogh Café and on your bill is a poem. What does it say? What future event does it reveal?

WRITER'S CRAFT

Opening Sentences

All good stories start with good opening sentences. After all, many people quit reading if their attention isn't caught right at the beginning of a story. Both *Lightning Strikes at the Van Gogh Café* and *A Wish Named Arnold* have excellent examples of opening sentences.

Reread both of these opening sentences, and with a partner discuss the information in them, and why the sentences are effective.

Try writing three opening sentences of your own. Choose the best one to develop into a complete story.

Fantastic Fiction

The last sentence of *Lightning Strikes at the Van Gogh Café* gives you a great idea for a fantasy story: magic muffins. But if magic food isn't your thing, why not write a fantasy story featuring some traditional fantasy creatures, such as unicorns, wizards, or talking animals?

Once you've written a final draft of your story, work with your classmates to develop a class collection of all the stories. Decide on a fantastic title for this collection, and ask the artists in the class to provide illustrations for the cover and all the stories.

TECH LINK

Post your stories on your school's Web site.

Something To Think About

Many traditional fantasy stories take place "long ago and far away," where it's easy to believe that magical things can happen. Charles de Lint and Cynthia Rylant have written fantasies about modern people, set in real places. Do you think it's easier or harder to write modern fantasy stories? Why?

Media Link · Fantasy Films

With your classmates, develop a movie guide for fantasy films. Think of fantasy movies you've seen, like *The Borrowers*, *The Neverending Story*, or *Quest for Camelot*. For each movie, write a note explaining what it was about. Was the movie animated, or did it use live actors? Who's the intended audience (children, adults, fantasy fans only)? Give each movie a rating (one, two, three, or four stars), and give your guide a catchy title. Share your fantasy movie guide with other classes, and family members.

Images are from the movies *Dragonheart* (top); *The Wizard of Oz* (middle); and *The Borrowers* (bottom).